Teaching Mindfulness to Children

A PRACTICAL GUIDE FOR PARENTS, TEACHERS, AND CAREGIVERS

Kelly Derouin and S. G. McKeever

McKEEVER PUBLISHING

SAN DIEGO   SAN FRANCISCO   FAIRFAX

ISBN: 978-1-885479-09-9

Cover design: Banalata Sundquist
Book formatting: Nicole Jones Sturk
Editing: Delaney Patterson

Printed in the United States of America
First printing August 2022

For additional information contact:
McKeever Publishing
P.O. Box 161167
San Diego, CA 92176

Table of Contents

Part I: Planting the Seeds of Mindfulness

Part II: Nurturing the Garden

Part III: Extra Nutrients

Part I

Planting the Seeds
of Mindfulness

1. Leading the Curve

There has never been a better time in history to sow the seeds of mindfulness in our hearts and in the hearts of our young ones. Amid a world of rapid flux and uncertainty, citizens of the global era—young and aging—need to know there exists a place of refuge, stability, and peace to be found within themselves. This book looks squarely at young people and sees in them the ideal practitioners of mindfulness. To develop as a human being who not only goes through the motions of life but also goes through those motions with self-awareness, self-acceptance, a healthy regard for others, and the belief that personal intention and mindful self-management can pave the path to personal joy— this is the promise of the mindful life.

Like the state of the world at large, childhood itself is a time of rapid growth, change, adaptation, learning, and challenges. Children who are shown how to access the calm, unwavering light of their inner beings have an immeasurable advantage in navigating childhood, cultivating healthy habits, and growing into their potentials as adults. A generally peaceful ride along the sometimes-rocky road of childhood *is* possible.

This book will guide you through guiding children how to center themselves in mindfulness and meditation practices. These practices include body-and-breath awareness, cognitive awareness and focus, creative visualizations, and self-reflection. We offer both theoretical, contextual information as well as practical, immediately usable lesson plans and scripting to help you share the techniques with confidence. The lesson plans and scripting are designed to guide children safely and swiftly to their inner tranquility. As the leader, you will guide children on that path to themselves. You will help them locate and connect with their natural states of well-being. This service you render may just be the gift of their lifetime.

Raising and working with children, whether as a parent, educator, caregiver, counselor, or social worker, is a huge job. Imagine passing to children a skillset that immensely benefits their well-being *and* makes your work in managing them easier, saner, and more balanced.

Leading the curve in offering this skillset to children may seem daunting, but you will find that results come speedily and steadily. Unruly as they are by nature, some children will take to the practice more readily than others. While most children enjoy resting, relaxing, listening to stories, closing their eyes, and imagining, others will require coaxing or perhaps your gentle acceptance that they may be either developmentally unready for or simply uninterested in mindfulness exercises.

If you are unfamiliar with meditation and mindfulness and have no practice of your own, fear not! This book will guide you in not only sharing mindfulness with children but also discovering the life-altering magic of cultivating a practice of your own. In essence, the techniques for children are not so different from that for adults.

In our experience, the habit of meditating for a few minutes prior to guiding the practice for others is a great idea. If possible, just a few moments of closing your eyes, quieting your mind, and taking a few relaxing belly breaths can fill your cup before you pour into others. Additionally, feel free to participate in the exercises yourself as you lead the techniques and read the scripts for others. In fact, doing so will increase the efficacy and enjoyment of the experience for both you and the children.

2. Why Do Children Need Mindfulness?

> I learned to meditate at age 17. I wished I had learned even earlier!
>
> –Sujantra

As you share these practices with children, it is good to periodically refuel your inspiration by reminding yourself of the *why* behind the work. Over time, this *why* will expand for you and bring a higher level of personal satisfaction to your efforts. In our work with children, we have gained one key insight that fuels our *why*, and it is this: The benefits of mindfulness and meditation can apply to anyone, at any time, and in nearly any place or set of circumstances. This skillset is vastly inclusive.

We might assume that only the children who are experiencing stress and anxiety or emerging from troubled backgrounds can benefit from the calming effects of mindfulness and meditation. This is not so. Children who come from secure, conscious, and loving backgrounds as well as children who are ahead of their peers in some regard—perhaps possessing rare gifts or aptitudes—can just as readily reap the rewards of mindfulness. No one is exempt from the possibility of inner peace and self-improvement through mindfulness and meditation.

For Children Experiencing Stress

All children, like all humans, experience stress from time to time. The main difference between childhood stress and adulthood stress is that children have fewer coping mechanisms for dealing with stress and a limited awareness of possible resolutions to stress. In other words, children are more vulnerable to the impacts of stress, which in turn can perpetuate more stress.

Children experiencing stress often respond most profoundly to these practices. Simply the exposure to the practices can alter their awareness in a positive way. Imagine, for example, a child who lives in a cramped and noisy home with dysfunctional family dynamics. Then, imagine this child is walking home from school one day and decides to stop and peek inside a place of worship he often passes. Inside the place of worship, he sees vaulted ceilings and magnificent spaciousness. There is a peaceful hush and quietude, ambient lighting from stained glass windows and candlelight, and a few persons interspersed in pews, kneeling calmly in prayer or meditation. This environment is entirely unlike what he is accustomed to. His eyes are now open to a new facet of reality.

This very example could be reconstructed as a visualization exercise, which is one of the methods we will detail in this book. We can guide children to peaceful places inside their imaginations. (In a classroom setting, you can determine the most appropriate imagery, of course. Scenes from nature are great, secular options.) Furthermore, we can prompt children to notice how they feel when they imagine these peaceful settings. This act of *noticing* and reflecting upon their responses is the act of mindfulness.

For Children at Ease

Children who are generally at ease present as calm, composed, and emotionally regulated. They are generally content and well-behaved. They do not demand exorbitant attention. For these reasons, we may overlook these children as candidates for mindfulness and meditation; after all, they are already seemingly blissed out! The truth is, these children benefit just as much from the opportunity to close their eyes, experience their inner worlds, and notice the natural processes of their bodies, such as breath flow, heartbeat, and the gifts of their senses.

Through meditation and mindfulness, we are introduced to ourselves. We enter our figurative temples and are reminded of our innate, individual essences, as layers of societal programming and conditioning are shed and left at the door. Children who consistently behave according to the standards set before them are—let's be honest—a real treat to work with! They are easier to manage. That said, it is possible that when you share mindfulness and meditation with these children, you help them unlock a door to exciting worlds within themselves, new possibilities, and a deeper appreciation of who they are at their core. Beneath their docility, they can be shown a safe space to engage and explore their inner worlds.

All children face challenges and stressors, even the most well-adjusted. It's not that we share mindfulness and meditation practices in anticipation of such stress—for these practices can be enjoyable, enlightening, and life-affirming just as they are. That said, these practices also lay groundwork for a sturdy sense of self that may be called upon during the inevitable, unforeseen challenges of life. This is even more reason to share mindfulness and meditation with children who seem to already enjoy a state of ease.

For Children Who Excel

Much like our attitudes regarding children who experience ease, we tend not to worry about children who excel and exceed. We see them as well on their way to achievement, success, and bright futures. In fact, many of them have already tasted peak experiences related to their advanced developmental capacities and feats. They often have attentive, supportive parents and adult figures cheering them on from the sidelines. They are celebrated and seen in a positive light. Since they have already found a measure of success, we may think the benefits of mindfulness and meditation may be only marginal or supplemental. But… not so fast! We would be mistaken to overlook these children as prime practitioners of mindfulness and meditation.

Children with exceptional intellectual abilities, for example, may relish in the opportunity to relax and slow their minds. It may be incredibly empowering for them to realize that they have a measure of control over their faculties of thought, feeling, and self-conduct. With practice, they can learn how and when to power on and power down these functions, offering them moments of rest, renewal, and relief from the urge to perform. Furthermore, they may learn that their self-worth and self-image need not hinge on their intellectual prowess. Beneath their exceptional abilities, they are important, worthy, and special for just being themselves.

Looking at this another way, children in their various states and circumstances may find that mindfulness and meditation is just the place to uncover and unleash their unique capacities and potentials for personal momentum. We have seen firsthand the bright, clear-eyed look of children who emerge from their meditations inspired and ready to act on some positive impulse. When the dust and clutter of everyday life are swept aside, the meditative mind often points its spotlight directly on the individual's gifts seeking to emerge.

3. Meet Your Teachers: Kelly and Sujantra

This book grew out of our experiences teaching workshops at Pilgrimage of the Heart Yoga in San Diego, California. We have worked with teachers, parents, grandparents, and social workers to guide them through sharing meditation and mindfulness with children.

Kelly Derouin

Hello, and welcome! Thank you for choosing to journey with us through these pages, where we hope to inspire you to take the leap into sharing mindfulness and meditation with children.

My appreciation for mindfulness began in college when I began practicing yoga. I was a theater major and very active physically. I found that this new practice of yoga helped me on multiple fronts: stress relief, finding peace of mind, getting in touch with my breath and body, and my overall concentration. As a musical theater performer, it helped me with my breath control while singing and dancing, as well as with my focus on stage.

After graduation, I began teaching performing arts. I was surprised to find how much I enjoyed teaching young people and witnessing their confidence bloom as they learned new ways to express themselves.

A few years later, I made the decision to become a certified yoga teacher. I studied at Pilgrimage of the Heart Yoga, where I was trained in meditation by Sujantra McKeever. Prior to that, I didn't have much of a meditation practice. In college, I had a philosophy professor who began his eight o'clock class with a ten-minute silent meditation; if I wasn't sleeping through it, then I was barging into the classroom late and disrupting it. Meditation always seemed like this big, scary, esoteric thing to me, and I met with some resistance to it when the practice was first introduced to me.

What I loved about Sujantra's approach to meditation was that it demystified the practice for me. His method of breaking it down step by step made the experience much less daunting and scary. Coming from a background of working with children, I saw the value of developing a mindfulness practice for myself, and I also saw the desperate need for it among the young people I worked with.

In my mind, the two art forms of mindfulness and performance arts complement each other beautifully. When teaching performing arts, I incorporate teachings of mindfulness, breath control, and focus. Likewise, when I teach yoga to young ones, I bring in storytelling, music, dance, and imagination. What I've seen with young people is that when they discover the magic of the breath, they undergo a complete transformation. What blossoms is their poise, their confidence, and their ability to fully share who they are and speak from the heart in front of others.

My inspiration has led me to programs such as the "Calm Kids" training with the Sean O'Shea Foundation, a foundation dedicated to bringing the practice of yoga to children in schools, particularly in underserved communities. I eventually founded my own children's yoga summer camp: Yoga Schmoga Kids Camp. I currently serve as the Director of Wellness at a private school in Southern California, where I work daily with preschool through fifth grade students.

The lesson plans and tips offered in this book are tried, true, and designed to be easily implemented at any level. We know they will serve you well.

Sujantra McKeever

Welcome! Thank you for being here and for endeavoring to bring meditation and mindfulness to young people. We have seen the vital effects these tools have had on the children we've worked with, and we hope this book will be a guide for you as you curate your own offerings to the children with whom you live or work.

My passion for sharing meditation with children originates in my own childhood experience with meditation. As a freshman in high school, I was—not unlike other high schoolers—plagued with self-consciousness in social environments. I became increasingly aware of unproductive self-talk and self-doubt in my mind, and I didn't know how to stop it. I noticed, however, that when I played sports, I was happy and relaxed.

My first experience with the calming effect of meditation came through breathwork. One of my older cousins trained me in long-distance running. He and I would go on three- and four-mile runs, and he would encourage me to relax and focus on my breathing. I remember how peaceful and happy I felt after those runs! I then learned to focus on my breathing while simply sitting quietly. That became the solution for me, across various activities and situations: concentrate on my breath and stay focused on positive thoughts.

Some of my earliest experience working with children was giving private tennis lessons. In these lessons, I offered visualization techniques and breathing exercises to help the children learn and have fun. In 1999, I opened Pilgrimage of the Heart Yoga and have since taught yoga and meditation to both adults and children through classes, extended trainings, and certification programs. I routinely travel to schools and offer these practices at the elementary through high school levels.

In teaching mindfulness and meditation to children, I've found it's always best to meet them where they're at. Simple breath awareness is a tool that can be used ubiquitously. I once worked with an 11-year-old student who was dealing with anxiety. I knew he loved basketball, so he and I went to a basketball court and started dribbling, passing, and shooting. As we played, I encouraged him to focus on his breathing as much as possible. Instead of worrying about whether the shot will go in, I advised, keep your primary focus on your breath. Shoot the shot but keep your thoughts on your breath.

As we continued to play, I saw a lightheartedness in his demeanor begin to take over. There were more grins and laughter and fewer furrowed expressions. There is nothing like watching a child transition from tension, anxiety, and debilitating self-talk to ease, playfulness, and self-confidence.

Mindfulness is an equal-opportunity activity. Regardless of which challenges or developmental phase the child may be navigating, each child can develop the skills and habits to benefit from the practice. For some, it may positively alter the trajectory of their entire lives. It did mine.

4. The Five Mindfulness Stepping Stones

Over many years of guiding adults and children through meditation, we have developed a five-step method to help students transition through the layers of mind-body awareness with ease. We call it the *Five Mindfulness Stepping Stones*. For children, the five-step process is adapted to three distinct age groups, which we'll discuss and lay out later in the book.

First, let's review the terms *meditation* and *mindfulness*. The two go hand in hand, but each carries subtle variations in meaning.

Meditation is, simply, the exploration of one's own mind. The meditation experience roots us in an awareness of our minds. The practice of meditation involves focusing the mind for a period of time, often in silence, and leads to varied states of mindfulness. In other words, meditation is a practice that engenders mindfulness.

Mindfulness is paying attention to the present moment. The attention given is intentional and non-judgmental. A person exercising mindfulness observes one's own body states, sensations, thoughts, and emotions in the present moment.[1] Mindfulness is to be exercised in many situations, not just meditative processes. Meditation, however, is a great place to discover and build the mindful muscle.

The concepts of meditation and mindfulness can be further grasped by the psychological term *metacognition*, which will appear throughout this text. Metacognition is *the awareness of one's own thinking*. Thinking is one thing, but observing the content, quality, and processes of one's own thought is another thing. Those skilled in metacognition can be seen as custodians of their own minds.

Metacognition takes us, for instance, from thinking a judgmental thought about the lady we see in the grocery store who is wearing an unconventional style of footwear to thinking, "I just passed judgment on the lady in the grocery store. Did that thought feel good or constructive to me? Was it a worthwhile use of mental energy? Was it kind? How does my body feel after thinking that thought?" Metacognition is one of the life-altering capacities developed through the practice of meditation.

With these definitions in mind, let's look at our five-step approach to meditation and mindfulness.

Creating the Environment

Surroundings and environment are significant when practicing the five steps. Before beginning the mindfulness process, consider the physical space the children occupy. Create an environment that is pleasant and calming for their senses.

Creating the Environment for Mindfulness

SIGHT

A visual focal point: a candle, flower, picture from nature, or window with a pleasant view.

SOUND

Calming instrumental music. Typing "meditation music" into any streaming service will result in a broad selection to choose from.

TOUCH

Comfortable, inviting furniture and props, such as pillows.

SMELL

The diffusion of essential oils. This can be a soothing signal to the children that it is time for mindfulness.

TASTE

A glass of water, tea, or juice at hand. This may help calm and focus the sense of taste.

Five Mindfulness Stepping Stones

1. ENERGY REGULATION

Move the body to work out the wiggles and begin to induce self-regulation of energy. This can include recess play time, yoga, sports, or seated movements linked to breath.

2. CONSCIOUS RELAXATION

Combine breath control and physical awareness to relax and still the body.

3. CONCENTRATION

Gather up awareness by focusing on breath, visual imagery, music, or a story.

4. MEDITATION

Root down in guided visualization. Use imagination and concentration to cultivate feelings of wellness, inspiration, mental clarity, personal goals, and more. Omit this step for early-childhood learners.

5. REFLECTION

Engage in a reflective, creative process such as journaling, discussing, or drawing to assimilate the powerful impacts of meditation. Allow mindfulness to infuse daily life.

The five steps are best conducted chronologically, though you will skip over a step or two depending on the age group you are working with—a state of deep meditation, for instance, is not accessible to most three-year-olds.

Let's explore the nuances of each of the five steps.

STEP 1   Energy Regulation

The first step is to energize the mind and body. This helps the children to shake out the wiggles and feel grounded yet uplifted. When children sit for too long, they become either restless or lethargic. Both states impede the ability to meditate and make boredom or sleep more likely. Energy-regulation exercises boost the students' awareness of their bodies and help them release physical tensions and mental chatter.

The simplest energizing techniques can be done while seated, including shoulder shrugs, gentle neck rolls, and a few arm movements, but young children love to get up and move around. Any type of safe and structured movement will do the trick, such as yoga postures or dance moves. If the children have just come in from playtime, then you can move right into step two.

STEP 2   Conscious Relaxation

Relaxation exercises help children to do just that: relax. While some children are developmentally able to *consciously* notice the relaxation that washes over them, others will simply benefit from the palpable relaxation that sweeps over them and the room.

In relaxation, we guide children to settle in and allow everyday tensions and stressors to melt away. Relaxation also lays the foundation for deeper concentration to follow. The children are prompted to tune out distractions from the outer world and begin to focus their gaze inward.

Simple breathing exercises are a wonderful way to induce this state of calm. For many, this portion of the experience will offer the most substantial effects.

STEP 3   Concentration

Once the children are energized and relaxed, it's time to practice focusing their awareness. They are ready to draw their concentration inward and become aware of bodily sensations. The constant flow of breath is an example of a bodily sensation.

The five senses of the body lend themselves perfectly to concentration exercises. The visual focal point of a candle or the auditory focal point of peaceful music can give the children something to focus on as they tune out the rest of the world.

No attempt is made to silence the mind during concentration. Rather, the children are encouraged to simply notice how their minds wander during the exercise. By merely noticing this mental movement, they are practicing mindfulness. When students find themselves drifting into thoughts, they learn to bring their attention back to the tactile sensation of breath or any other sensation upon which they are focused. This focal point anchors the students' attention and awareness in the present moment.

Sight is an excellent basis for concentration. Research has shown that as much as 50% of the sensing brain is wired for sight.[2] When offering multiple exercises based on the physical senses, we typically do a vision exercise first, followed by an auditory exercise, and then exercises that engage the senses of touch, smell, and taste.

When using hearing as the basis for concentration, you may have students focus on the *sound* of their breathing rather than the tactile sensation of breathing. Using *touch* as the basis, you may have them ignore the sound of their breathing and instead concentrate on the tactile sensations of breath, such as the rise and fall of the belly.

Continuing with sound, you may guide your students to listen carefully as they recite a word or phrase either audibly or in silence. Repeated recitation is the essence of *mantra* meditation. Any voiced idea can be a mantra, even if it is voiced silently within the mind. Mantras can be a single syllable, a word, or a phrase. You can repeat a mantra in three ways: first, aloud, and sometimes in unison with others; second, silently but with your tongue forming the words; and third, silently with a motionless tongue and fully engaged mind. In silent recitation, there is still a mental sensation of sound.

Here are examples of focal points for concentration, both internal and external:

Sight
Outer: an actual candle flame
Inner: an imagined candle flame

Sound
Outer: vocal recitation of a mantra
Inner: silent recitation

Touch
Outer: real sand beneath the feet
Inner: memory of the sensation of sand

Smell
Outer: the scent of a lemon
Inner: a memory of scent

Taste
Outer: actual taste on the tongue
Inner: a memory of flavor

STEP 4 Meditation

When the children are at ease physically and focused mentally, it is time to guide them through a meditation, which often takes the form of visualization. A guided visualization directs students to use the power of imagination to move themselves into focused states of awareness. They can apply their focus toward experiencing simple peace of mind and body, cultivating qualities such as tenderness and courage, gaining insights about their lives, or projecting themselves into desired futures.

In essence, guiding a visualization exercise with children is just like reading a story to them. You provide the backbone of the story while they fill in the details with their imaginations. Give students space and freedom to choose colors, scenes in nature, and other aspects— this gives them the opportunity to make personal choices, own the experience, and infuse it with what is meaningful and relevant to them. For example, you might say, "Imagine a beautiful scene in nature, either a place you have been, a picture you have seen, or just use your imagination. Now imagine the colors of this scene... Notice how you feel in this peaceful place..."

When creating guided visualizations, include as many of the senses as possible. Be sure to use sight, sound, and touch, with taste and smell being optional, so that the experience is immersive and impactful. We offer several exercises in Part Two.

At the end of the meditation, always allow a few minutes for students to transition out of their individual experiences. Give them advance notice that the meditation will end in a couple minutes and suggest that they begin concluding whichever technique they are engaged in. After this transition period, slowly guide their awareness toward the external surroundings while suggesting they keep some of their awareness on the inner feelings or inspiration they received from their meditation.

The conclusion of the meditation exercise is not the end of the experience. Students must learn to integrate the benefits of their meditative experiences into their day-to-day lives. Feeling peace within or finding the inspiration to envision life in a new way can naturally flow into outer activity. In fact, this is the whole point of meditation! We meditate to enhance our quality and enjoyment of life and our relationships with self and others.

If time permits, encourage students to write down thoughts or feelings they experienced during meditation, especially positive ones. Some may prefer to draw, write a poem, or play an instrument. Any form of tangible self-expression is a wonderful way to integrate and reflect upon the meditative experience. This is mindfulness in action.

If the children envisioned themselves doing something new in their meditation, such as learning to play a musical instrument, then you can brainstorm with them as to how they may make that happen, and then check in with them on their progress. In many respects, everything that we accomplish and become in life begins with an idea in our minds. This is what makes meditation and mindfulness so transformative—they increase our awareness and our capacity to envision the lives we desire.

A Lifelong Practice

I've practiced meditation for 40 years, and I still use these same five stepping stones in my daily practice.

Every morning, I spend thirty minutes in meditation. It begins with ten minutes of spiritual, uplifting reading to get me out of my mundane thoughts, then a few minutes of stretching and breathing exercises, followed by whichever concentration and meditation techniques I am drawn to that morning. My meditation may be focused on sorting through challenges I will be facing that day, empathizing with a co-worker's situation, or envisioning how to move forward with a project.

Meditation is your time to empower your life. When you teach meditation and mindfulness to children, you teach them self-empowerment.

– Sujantra

5. Stages of Childhood Development

Guiding children through meditation and mindfulness becomes easier when you have a sense of their developmental capacities: physical, social, and cognitive. Part Two explores these capacities according to three age groups: early, middle, and later childhood.

The idea is to engage children in a way that honors where they are. For early- and middle-childhood students, the warmth, kindness, and consistency of your presence will be enough to create a foundation of safety and trust. Later-childhood students will be looking for authenticity and candor in your delivery, along with an ability to exercise your authority with goodwill.

Our approach draws heavily from the work of Jean Piaget (1896-1980), the Swiss psychologist known for his groundbreaking theory of childhood cognitive development. His theory is centered in the idea that children exhibit distinct, predictable patterns of cognition based on their ages and stages of development. Though Piaget cleaved childhood into four distinct phases, we will explore only three of them in this book. Piaget's first stage, from birth to age two, is not conducive to learning mindfulness.

Please note that while this book is organized to align teachers and parents with the age-specific information that is relevant to them, it can be illuminating to review the information for the other groups, as well. Not all children develop at the same rate. Some will be able to grasp only the techniques of an earlier stage, and some will need to explore techniques beyond their developmental category to stay engaged.

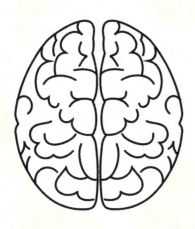

PIAGET'S STAGES OF COGNITIVE DEVELOPMENT

EARLY CHILDHOOD/ PRE-OPERATIONAL STAGE

2-7 years

Those in early childhood have a worldview that is limited to themselves and those immediately surrounding them. They are always engaged in present-moment awareness. They begin to understand symbols and love to play pretend. They do not yet understand logic, such as cause and effect. Their language skills are expanding rapidly.

MIDDLE CHILDHOOD/ CONCRETE OPERATIONAL STAGE

7-11 years

Children this age are capable of logical thought processes, but they understand things concretely, not in the abstract. They grasp the difference between appearance and reality, that actions can be reversed, and the law of conservation. Their worldview expands, and they begin to show empathy for others in scenarios they can personally relate to.

LATER CHILDHOOD/ FORMAL OPERATIONAL STAGE

11-18 years

Young people in this age group are capable of abstract and hypothetical thought. They are capable of creative problem solving, deductive reasoning, and metacognition. They can feel and show empathy in a wide variety of circumstances.

Part II

Nurturing the Garden

Here we address the characteristics and needs of children according to three age groups: Early Childhood (ages 2-7), Middle Childhood (7-11), and Later Childhood (11-18). Each chapter discusses the developmental phase of the respective age group, continues with strategies for guiding that group through mindfulness activities, and then concludes with lesson plans and scripting.

The lessons follow the *Five Mindfulness Stepping Stones* method presented in Chapter 4 and are designed for formal educational settings, but they are by no means rigid formulas. Please adapt them to your situation and know that completing all five steps is not always necessary. For example, you might do a three-minute conscious relaxation exercise with the children after they come in from recess, or you might do a simple meditation with your child as he or she lies in bed before sleep. A simple one-minute breathing exercise can help a child immensely.

As a general note: There will always be moments when your perfectly planned lesson gets interrupted. A child may act disruptively or refuse to participate. Try to incentivize and re-inforce the positive behavior first. For instance, instead of saying, "Alex, please stop talking out of turn and distracting your neighbor," try saying, "Wow, I love how Meghan is sitting so quietly on her mat and following instructions!" or "I'm looking for a volunteer to help me lead the breathing exercise. I'll call on someone who is sitting crisscross applesauce with their hands in their lap wearing a big smile."

If you have made several attempts to redirect distracting behavior, then it may help to have a private word with that child. Acknowledge that maybe this isn't his or her "thing" and that is OK, but it is not OK to be disrespectful and prevent classmates from participating. Then, offer the child another option you find acceptable. "If you don't feel like playing Musical Mats with us, then you may sit quietly on your mat and use the breathing ball for a few minutes," or, "You may lie down to relax or write quietly in your journal, but if you make too much noise and distract others from their relaxation, then you will need to wait outside until we are done."

The Child in Each of Us

Deep down, we each have our childhood selves inside of us and can get tremendous benefit from these techniques. One of the things I really enjoy when teaching workshops is doing the exercises myself and watching other participating adults get so much joy and relaxation from techniques that were developed for 2- to 7-year-olds!

In the *Thunderstorm* lesson plan, you will use your tapping fingertips to simulate the feeling of rain drops. I have used this technique in my business life. Whenever I am in a meeting and notice I am losing my concentration or composure, I start tapping my fingers on the top of the opposite hand or my thigh and imagine they are raindrops. It quickly brings me back into focus.

– Sujantra

6. Early Childhood (Ages 2–7)

Children ages two to seven are in early childhood, what Piaget called the *preoperational* stage. Let's explore some developmental milestones unique to this age group.

Physical Development

At ages two to three, children are developing their gross motor skills, which include jumping, crawling, pushing, and stacking toys. By ages four to seven, children can engage in finer motor skills that require longer attention spans, such as coloring, crafting, and cutting. Bear in mind that young children have limited body and spatial awareness until about six or seven years old. When playing physical games and doing energy-regulation activities that include dancing or running around, be sure to clear all furniture or objects out of the way. Because they are not fully aware of how their bodies move through space, they could potentially injure themselves or others.

Social Development

Socially speaking, children within this age group have an egocentric view of the world, which is not to say that they are full of themselves, but rather that their worldview is limited in scope. Their entire world is mom, dad, maybe a teacher, and a handful of playmates. They are the center of their universe and not yet able to take on another's point of view.

Cognitive Development

Early-childhood students are not yet cognitively able to think in the abstract. They understand the world in concrete shapes and forms. Ask a four-year-old, "What is love?" and the answer will likely be, "Love is your heart." A heart shape is a physical representation of an invisible concept. The child cannot form a mental concept, but he or she can draw the shape and know that it is associated with a positive feeling.

While early-childhood learners cannot grasp abstract ideas, they do engage in *symbolic play*. Hand a child a broom and say, "This is a unicorn. Let's go for a ride," and he or she will engage with no questions asked. Using toys as symbols to explain larger concepts will be a successful approach with this age group. For example, shake up a jar of glitter (see craft recipe at the end of Lesson 4) to demonstrate how our minds can sometimes get all jumbled with thoughts and feelings, but when we set down the jar and let it be still, all the glitter calms down and we can see through it clearly. If the children can see it and touch it in the real world, then they can make sense of its deeper meaning.

Language development is a hallmark for this age group. They learn new words every day, and their ability to communicate and express themselves grows drastically. Two-year-olds can speak in two-word sentences and may have a vocabulary of about fifty words, whereas five-year-olds can understand adult conversation, use past, present, and future tenses correctly, can count to ten, and knows left from right.

Children this age are only beginning to grasp basic logic, such as cause and effect. Children discover and explore these concepts through play and experimentation. For example, if a toy is thrown across the room or dropped, then it may break. They do not understand, however, that it can also likely be fixed. Because of their limited understanding, they may have strong emotional reactions to what an adult may see as a minor situation.

While they do not fully grasp logic and reason, their imaginations are vibrant and wild. As a teacher, you can best reach them through storytelling, imagination, and playfulness.

After the activities, don't expect lengthy reflection or profound discussion. Since children in this age range are developing their language skills, they may not be able to verbally reflect on their practice. They are incapable of metacognition and drawing deep connections; their minds simply are not there yet. However, coloring or crafting is a wonderful way to reflect. It is valuable to give them a buffer zone after the activities to experience their bodies and feelings.

The *Hand Model of the Brain* is an effective tool for this age group. It helps them understand how their brain works and why they feel and behave as they do. See Part Three for the graphic.

Toys As Tools

It can be extremely helpful to have sensory toys on hand, to serve as anchors of focus. I will never forget the instance when I had a second grade boy with a neurodevelopmental disorder in my wellness class. He had become known among his teachers and peers for his drastic mood changes and big emotional outbursts at minor triggers. My wellness class had just completed a successful yoga lesson followed by a short relaxation, but in the final moments of class, he was not called upon to share his reflection. He immediately melted down in screams and tears. I excused the rest of the class and tried desperately to talk him down. He was inconsolable. Since there was not much I could say at this point, I simply handed him my Hoberman Sphere, a toy we use as our "breathing ball," and watched as he slowed his breathing and self-soothed without a single word of guidance from me. This was eye-opening for me. I could not calm this child. I had to give him the tools and allow him to calm himself.

– Kelly

Guiding Strategy

Keep exercises short and simple. Change up the game often, or they will lose interest. Every little thing they perceive in the world is a new discovery they are witnessing for the first time. While children this young have a naturally short attention span, they are always engaged in the present moment, which means they are already some of the most mindful among us!

1. Energy Regulation

It's important for these little ones to get their wiggles out, so do an energy exercise that allows them to run around, move their bodies, and make lots of noise.

Encourage play with others. While this age group is naturally self-centered and not yet inclined to empathize or entertain another's perspective, they are developing social skills that will prepare them for school and the rest of the world. Any opportunity you give them to interact constructively with their peers is valuable.

2. *Conscious Relaxation*

When it's time to listen and focus, give them tools to calm down their bodies. Rather than saying, "It's time to calm down," help them understand what they need to do physically and emotionally to achieve what you are asking of them, perhaps most effectively by demonstrating it yourself. Calming breath exercises are simple and effective here.

3. *Concentration (and Meditation)*

Focused attention for any amount of time is equivalent to meditation for this group. Do not expect the children to be still or quiet, have their eyes closed, or practice for lengthy periods of time. A practice may be silly, noisy, and last only two minutes, and that is a successful mindfulness practice for this age group.

Guide them to focus for a few breaths or a couple minutes. Early-childhood students need visuals and tactile anchors to help them focus, so use lots of toys and props. Some notable examples are feathers, straws, a Hoberman sphere, pinwheels, stuffed animals, play dough, glitter jars, and anything visually mesmerizing or sensory. You can also have them focus on the sound of your voice as you read them a story.

4. *Reflection*

There are many ways to reflect with students who are still developing their verbal skills. You can ask them for a simple thumbs up or thumbs down if they felt good or if they liked that experience. You can ask them to show you a number on their fingers; "One through five, how much did you like that experience? One, I didn't like it. Five, I loved it." You can ask them to share one word for how they feel in this moment, or "If you were a color, what color do you feel like right now?"

These reflections engage their thinking and allow them to reflect on how they are feeling without using too advanced a vocabulary. It is valuable for them not only to take a moment to think about it but also to self-determine and to share openly about how they are feeling. This is a wonderful primer in learning how to verbalize what they are experiencing.

Lesson Plan #1

Lesson: "Feather Fun!"　　　**Time: 20-30 minutes**
Age group: 2-7 year olds

Goals: Teach breath awareness and self-soothing relaxation techniques

Materials Needed:

One feather per child
If you do not have feathers, you can tear a small scrap of paper to use as a feather.

SEL Core Competencies:

- Self-Awareness
- Self-Management
- Responsible Decision Making

1. Energy Regulation

Let's play a game where we make our feathers float! Everyone, toss your feather up in the air and using only your breath, blow air out of your mouth to keep the feather floating in the air. No hands! Who can keep their feather floating the longest?

Now let's try a feather race! Everyone pair up with a partner and we'll all take turns laying our feather down on the "starting line." When I say "GO!" you and your partner will blow as hard as you can, as many times as it takes to move your feathers across the "finish line." Whose feather will be the fastest?

2. Conscious Relaxation

Wow! It was so cool to see how you could move your feather around the room using only the power of your breath. Let's take a few minutes to focus in closely on how our breath moves the feather.

Hold your feather in front of your face. Take a nice deep breath in through your nose and let out a long sigh from your mouth. What did your feather do? Let's try that a couple more times. Did you see the feather move back and forth as you were breathing?

Now we'll practice breathing in and out of the nose, nice and easy. Do you see the feather moving still?

3. Concentration

This little feather has magic powers! We are going to use it to help our minds and bodies relax and focus.

Sit or lie down comfortably and close your eyes. Take your magic feather in one hand and begin to lightly trace the tip of that feather on your other hand. Does that tickle? It's ok to have a good giggle if you need to, but let's stay focused on the feeling of that magic feather tracing along our skin.

Let the tip of your feather move up and down your arm, over your shoulder, across your chest, maybe down over your belly and legs, or up over your neck and face. Every part of your body that this feather touches becomes calm, still, and relaxed.

4. Reflection

- What was your favorite feather activity that we did today?

- Give me a thumbs up if you liked the magic feather games, thumbs down if you did not, and a halfway thumb if you're not sure.

- Raise your hand and tell me one word that describes how you feel right now, after our magic feather exercise.

- Your magic feathers have the power to calm and relax you whenever you need. Can you think of a time when you might use your magic feather to help you calm down? When you feel super duper excited? When you feel nervous? When you feel out of control angry, perhaps?

Optional Craft: Feather Necklaces!

Additional supplies: colorful paper, beads, string or yarn, tape.

Let's use our magic feathers to make necklaces, so we can take our feather and its calming magic powers wherever we go!

Tape the feather to the colorful paper. Attach it to a string with beads and tie it all together to form a simple necklace.

Lesson Plan #2

Lesson: "Thunderstorm" **Time: 20-30 minutes**
Age group: 2-7 year olds

Goals: Release body tension, slow the breath, teach self-awareness.

Materials Needed:

Copy of "Storm Starters" Worksheet (one per child) and writing utensils

SEL Core Competencies:

- Self-Awareness
- Social Awareness
- Self-Management
- Responsible Decision Making

1. Energy Regulation

Our emotions can sometimes feel like a thunderstorm: loud, powerful, and out of control. Can any of you think of a time when you felt "out of control" with a big emotion? Today we'll create that feeling of a thunderstorm.

Sit down comfortably. We'll begin by lightly tapping our fingers on top of our heads. It almost feels like little rain drops falling on our heads, doesn't it? Close your eyes and enjoy that feeling.

Now the raindrops will travel down the sides of our faces and onto the tops of our shoulders, then maybe over our chests. The rain is getting faster and louder as it goes. The rain is getting so strong now, that instead of tapping our fingers we'll use our palms to pat the tops of our legs. Hear that big sound? It's like heavy rain!

We have a big rainstorm happening now. Maybe we'll hear some thunder by pounding our fists on the ground or a table for a second. Maybe we'll hear the crack of lightening by clapping our hands together. Make a big loud thunderstorm everybody!

Now the worst of the storm is over, and the thunder and lightning are gone. The rain begins to lessen, so pat your bodies with your fingers again instead of your palms. The fingers tap all the way back up to the top of your head and then begin to gradually slow down.

2. Conscious Relaxation

After that thunderstorm we created with our bodies, let's begin to focus on our breathing and see if we can create the sound of calming ocean waves.

Breathe in through your nose, and breathe out through your nose, making a gentle hissing sound at the back of your throat, as if you were whispering or trying to fog up a mirror with your breath. Close your eyes and listen closely to the ebb and flow of your breath, just like the waves of the ocean. If it's difficult to hear, place your hands over your ears for a few rounds and really tune in. Did you hear it that time? Let's take five more deep breaths.

3. Concentration

Now let's lie down comfortably. Close your eyes and continue listening to the sound of your ocean breath. Imagine you are floating atop the waves of the ocean. See the clear blue sky above. Feel the warmth of the sun on your face and the cool touch of the water on your skin. Take a deep breath and smell the salty sea air. Maybe you even hear a seagull calling as it flies by.

With every breath, your body floats up and down. Your body is perfectly safe, comfortable, and relaxed.

4. Reflection

- How did you feel when you were in the middle of the Thunderstorm activity in the beginning of the lesson? Tense? Excited? Overwhelmed?

- How do you feel now after the Ocean Drift exercise? Calm? Quiet? Sleepy?

Optional Craft: Storm Starters Worksheet

Using the Storm Starters Worksheet, help the students to identify things that trigger them to feel a storm of emotions. Then, write down how that emotion may cause them to react. If they are still learning to write, they can dictate to you what they want to say or draw a picture instead. Finally, work together to figure out a helpful way to respond when faced with these emotions.

For example, "I get angry when something is too hard. Instead of getting frustrated and giving up, I can take a break and practice ocean breath until I'm ready to try again."

Storm Starters!
self-awareness and self-regulation

EMOTIONAL TRIGGER	MY REACTION	WHAT I CHOOSE TO DO INSTEAD
 Example: I miss a goal during soccer practice.	 I get angry, yell, and quit the game.	 I choose to take five deep breaths, remind myself that I am still learning, and try again.

7. Middle Childhood (Ages 7–11)

Middle childhood includes children ages seven to eleven and is what Piaget referred to as the *concrete operational* stage. Here are key points to remember when working with this group.

Physical Development

By the elementary school years, children's physical movements are more coordinated, diverse, and controlled. They may be participating in sports, dance, gymnastics, or martial arts, and they are certainly participating in physical education (P.E.) at school. They have a lot of energy and are always on the move.

Social Development

This age group becomes more social and influenced by peers. Their worldview broadens to include friends and acquaintances outside of their immediate family unit. As their world expands, they begin to demonstrate empathy and the ability to see another's perspective. This ability is still limited, however, to scenarios they have personally experienced and can relate to. For example, "Greg fell on the playground, and I know how that feels because I once fell on the playground and scraped my knee."

Cognitive Development

These children are capable of logical thought, including cause and effect and the consequences of action. "If I go outside in the rain without my coat on, I will get wet." They understand, too, that actions can be reversed. For instance, if a toy is accidentally dropped, it may break, but it can likely be fixed. They generally understand the law of conservation, meaning that a thing can change shape and still retain its identity, e.g., if a candy bar breaks in half, it is still a candy bar but now in two pieces, and it can still be eaten. If a cup of water is poured into two smaller cups, it is the same amount of water but in smaller cups.

They are not yet fully capable of abstract and hypothetical thought, but they can make logical connections and use reasoning. Ask a ten-year-old, "What is love?" and he or she will likely answer, "Love is what I feel for my mom and dad." Mom and dad here represent something more complex than the shape of a heart understood by early-childhood learners (see Chapter 6), but mom and dad still represent a basic, familiar, and concrete relationship that the child has experienced and can articulate.

Guiding Strategy

A great method for engaging this group is to *play* rather than to *teach*. In other words, don't think of yourself as a teacher who is there to teach them how to be healthy, but rather as a playmate who has a fun new game for them to try.

1. Energy Regulation

Allow them to shake out their wiggles and jitters. Encourage them to release physical, emotional, and mental tensions through purposeful movement.

2. Conscious Relaxation

Guide them to ground and calm their bodies and minds in the present moment. Be forewarned, they can become competitive and sometimes overzealous with their breathing exercises; advise them not to force anything and to take it slowly. Between breathing exercises, take a few moments for normal breathing.

3. Concentration

This age group can focus for several minutes. An estimate for concentration exercises is 7–15 minutes in length. That said, be flexible and willing to change things up. Depending on the mood of the day and other factors, some concentration sessions will last longer than others.

4. Meditation

Allow concentration to flow directly into meditation. This can take the form of a visualization. Remember, any amount of focused attention for any length of time is a successful meditation.

5. Reflection

Always end practice with a period of reflection. You can expect the children in this age group to be able to verbalize and write in complete sentences about how they are feeling.

In our experience, this age group is the most talkative and eager to express themselves. If you lead them through a guided visualization, they will want to tell you all about the Ice Cream Mountain they climbed and the Sparkly Rainbow Tree they sat under. If you taught them a new yoga pose, they will cry out, "Mom, mom, mom, see? I'm doing it!" If something you said triggered a memory of when they went on a hike through the forest with their grandmother, they will share the whole story with you. Allot ample time for these reflections.

Ask them specific questions to help them draw connections between their thoughts, feelings, and the exercises. Example prompts: How did you feel before the practice? How do you feel now, afterwards? What was your favorite part?

Lesson Plan #3

Lesson: "Magic Musical Mats"   Time: 45-60 minutes
Age group: 7-11 year olds

Goals: Balance energy levels, stimulate imagination and focus, teach self-awareness.

Materials Needed:

Yoga or exercise mats
(one per child) and a device to play music.

SEL Core Competencies:

- Self-Awareness
- Self-Management

1. Energy Regulation

(If you know yoga, have the children set up their yoga mats in a circle. Start by teaching 5-10 simple yoga poses that are easy to remember. If you are unfamiliar with yoga, you can look up simple postures ahead of time. **Suggested poses: Tree, Downward Dog, Cobra, Triangle, Warrior 1 or 2, Butterfly, Boat, and Dancer.** Another option is to play any form of musical chairs.)

Let's play a game called Musical Mats! It's just like Musical Chairs but with a fun yoga twist! Everyone starts by standing on their own yoga mat. I'll play some music, and while the music is playing, you all can dance and hop from mat to mat. When the music stops, I'll call out the name of one of the yoga poses we learned, and you all strike the pose!

(If you want to make it more competitive, the last person to make the yoga pose is out and removes their mat from the circle.)

2. Conscious Relaxation

Now let's lie down on our yoga mats. Start by lying on your belly, face forward, resting your forehead on your hands or with your head turned to one side. Close your eyes and let your breathing slow down to its natural rhythm. Do you feel your belly pressing into the floor every time you inhale? Then, feel your whole body relax each time you exhale. Focus on the feeling of your breath for another 5-10 breaths.

2. Conscious Relaxation (continued)

Now we'll roll over so we're lying on our left sides. You can rest your head on your arm. Notice where your midsection is now touching the mat. Can you breathe into that part of your body so that you feel it pressing into the floor just like before? Let's try it for five breaths.

Very good! Last, we'll roll over onto our backs. Rest your hands on top of your belly and continue to breathe slowly and evenly. Do you feel how your belly moves up and down with each breath? Let's focus on the up and down rhythm for 5-10 breaths.

3. Concentration

If you haven't already, close your eyes. Now, imagine that the yoga mat lying beneath you is a magic carpet. What colors is your mat? Does it have a special design? Feel the texture of its fabric. Is it soft and fluffy? Smooth? Or scratchy?

Your magic carpet begins to lift you off the floor, and you are hovering in midair, but no need to worry. Your magic carpet will keep you safe and supported no matter what. As your magic carpet lifts you and begins to carry you up and out the window, you feel the air breeze past your face. You hear the outside world moving around you, maybe the sound of birds singing, cars driving, people talking far beneath you. Your carpet takes you up higher and higher, above the treetops and buildings, above the clouds even. Reach out your hands and touch a soft, fluffy, white cloud. Maybe even open your mouth as you drift through the cloud. Does it have a taste? Over your head you see the deep blue sky. You smell the crisp clean air as you sail through space, and you feel the warmth of the sun on your body.

You feel your magic carpet begin to lower you down again, but now you are in a whole new place. This is a place that you love, that makes you feel safe and happy. It may be a place that you recognize and know very well, or it may be a magical fantasy place that no one knows but you.

3. Concentration (continued)

Look around. Notice the colors and shades of light. Is it daytime or nighttime here? Do you hear anything? Music? The voices of people you love? Take a nice deep breath in through your nose. Do you smell a specific scent? Maybe flowers, or perfume, or the smell of your favorite food cooking? Reach out your hand and touch a surface here. What does it feel like to you? This is your own special happy place. You can stay here as long as you like.

When you're ready, take one last look around and say goodbye to your happy place. It will always be here for you, and you can come back to visit any time you want. Climb back onto your magic carpet and lie down. Feel it lift you up again and carry you up through the clouds, through the sky, and back down over the familiar treetops and buildings. You drift back in through the window and feel your magic carpet set you gently back down on the floor in this room.

Slowly begin to wiggle your fingers and toes. Stretch your arms and legs, maybe have a nice yawn. And when you're ready, blink your eyes open and sit on up.

4. Reflection

- Would anyone like to share something they experienced on their magic carpet ride? Where did you go? What did you see?
- How did your magic carpet ride make you feel?
- How do you feel now, after our meditation practice, compared to in the middle of our Musical Mats game when we were running around and playing? Do you notice a difference?
- What was your favorite exercise that we did today? Why?

Lesson Plan #4

Lesson: "Glitter and Color"   **Time: 45-60 minutes**
Age group: 7-11 year olds

Goals: Balance energy levels, teach body and breath awareness, and calming techniques.

Materials Needed:

Glitter Jar or Snow Globe (optional), additional materials needed for craft

SEL Core Competencies:

- Self-Awareness
- Self-Management
- Responsible Decision Making

1. Energy Regulation

(Show the students your glitter jar/snow globe. Pass it around so they can each take turns shaking it up and watching it swirl. If you don't have one, you can find a glitter jar video online, or have the students close their eyes and visualize one.)

See this glitter jar everyone? This jar represents our mind, and the glitter swirling around in it is our thoughts and emotions. It's easy for our thoughts and feelings to get all shaken up, but when we set down the glitter jar/snow globe for a while and let it be still, our mind can become clear. Let's try it ourselves!

Everyone, please stand up. We are going to shake out our bodies. Let's start with our right hand. Raise it up and shake it as fast as you can. Do this for about 30 seconds. Now let's do the same with the left hand. Right foot. Left foot. Shoulders. Elbows. Knees. Head. Now shake your whole entire body! Shake harder and faster!

Whew! Ok, let's slow down and rest our arms and legs. Stand up tall and close your eyes for a moment. How do you feel? Tired? Tingly? Warm? We certainly stirred things up!

2. Conscious Relaxation

Now come to a comfortable position sitting or lying down. We're going to relax every part of our bodies. Focus on your hands once again. Squeeze your fingers into the shape of a fist and hold them as tight as you can for 5-4-3-2-1. Now release and let your hands be as loose as a pair of floppy old socks.

Let's do the same with our feet. Curl your toes and give them a good squeeze for 5-4-3-2-1, then release and let your feet flop open.

Close your eyes and squeeze them tight. Scrunch your nose and mouth together. Curl your whole body up into a tight little ball, hugging your knees. Take a deep breath. Now open your mouth, stretch out your body, and let everything relax as you breathe out.

3. Concentration

As you let your body rest, imagine that you are soaking in a bathtub of warm bubbly water. But this isn't just any water; it is your favorite color! Picture yourself taking a bath in your favorite color paint.

Now imagine your favorite color dripping off your body and soaking into the floor beneath you as you rest here. Think of the parts of your body that are touching the floor right now: your legs, your back, your shoulders, and head. The paint that drips off these parts of your body forms a colored shape of you! What might that shape look like?

When you're ready, slowly roll your body over to one side and press up to a comfortable seat. Keep your eyes closed and imagine all that paint sliding off your skin and settling back down on the floor. Your body is clean, and your mind is clear, just like that glitter jar after we let it rest for a while.

4. Reflection

- Who would like to share what color paint they imagined?
- What kinds of thoughts and feelings might be swirling around in your glitter jar today?
- What situations make you feel all shaken up inside?
- How can you help your glitter/thoughts and feelings settle when they are stirred up?

Optional Craft: Glitter Jars!

Additional Supplies: glass jars or recycled plastic bottles, clear glue, glitter, food coloring, water

Let's make glitter jars of our own that we can use to help calm our minds when we feel shaken up.

Fill the jars or bottles almost all the way full with water. Add a few drops of food coloring and a large squeeze of clear glue. The more glue, the slower the glitter will move. Then add in the glitter and stir it all up well. Glue the lid of the jar or bottle on tight and enjoy!

8. Later Childhood (Ages 11–18)

Later childhood, ages eleven to eighteen, is referred to as the *formal operational* stage. Children in this age group want to be seen and treated as adults, and in many ways—physically and cognitively—they can be considered young adults. Here are key points to consider.

Physical Development

A huge amount of physical change and growth happens during the preteen and teenage years. Bodies mature rapidly. Systems are flooded with hormones. Preteens and teens experience new feelings and bodily sensations that they are sometimes unsure how to manage, and they become more self-conscious.

While this age group is the most physically coordinated, they may be hesitant to participate in a physical activity if they fear it will cause them embarrassment.

Social Development

Empathy is now fully accessible. At this stage in life, the brain has developed enough to identify with others' perspectives. A child can imagine how someone might think or feel, without having experienced it for him- or herself. Should you witness any unempathetic behavior in this age group, you can challenge them to call upon their powers of empathy to rethink their response.

Cognitive Development

This group is capable of abstract and hypothetical thinking. You can ask them open-ended, theoretical questions and receive interesting, thought-provoking answers. They are skilled in creative problem solving and deductive reasoning. Expect them to figure out things on their own and solve their own problems. Ask a sixteen-year-old, "What is love?" and he or she may compose a song, sculpt an abstract art piece, or write a persuasive essay on the subject.

Metacognition, the ability to examine one's own thoughts and thought processes, becomes possible at this stage. Children in this group can observe and challenge their ways of thinking. The *Hand Model of the Brain* and the *Sun of Awareness* are appropriate frameworks to explore with this group. While the *Hand Model of the Brain* is a straightforward visual representation, the *Sun of Awareness* requires the skill of metacognition, challenging them to practice viewing their selves, thoughts, feelings, and behaviors from an observational standpoint.

Guiding Strategy

It is paramount that this age group disconnects from all electronic devices during the mindful experience. Give them a distraction-free space to practice. Perhaps provide a box or designated area where all students place their mobile devices at the beginning of class. Model for them by turning off your own device and setting it aside so you can be fully present with them.

Ensure a comfortable and safe environment so they are willing to be vulnerable with you. Room setup can include dim lighting, calming colors, and soft, comforting surfaces like blankets and pillows. Avoid mirrors if you can. You can set up the room so that everyone sits in a circle to feel equal and engaged, or you can have them set up individually in any area of the room where they feel comfortable. A personal bubble fosters a sense of freedom and personal choice, which—paradoxically—can bolster cooperation among teenagers.

For these older students, a key method to establishing credibility is to share with them why you started meditating. Express vulnerabilities or challenges you faced that led you to meditation. Share specific examples of changes or transformations that occurred in your life because of practicing meditation. The more honest your expression, the more your students will resonate with your offering. Presenting yourself as a human being with strengths and weaknesses will give the students confidence to be beginners.

This age group may not respond as well to *playing* as the early- and middle-childhood stages do. They prefer to be treated more maturely and challenged in novel ways. Though they are not fully adults, their brains are quickly growing and transforming into adult brains. Often, the activities used for younger students can be adapted to fit the needs of older children simply by presenting them with a more advanced vocabulary and emphasizing the mature skillset needed to engage in the activities.

1. Energy Regulation

In our experience, this age group does not need to get the wiggles out. Rather, they need to shake off lethargy and wake themselves up.

2. Conscious Relaxation

Guide them to calm themselves, to stay alert and present, and to let go of tension that may have crept into their systems. Young adults tend to be under various forms of stress, so this practice of conscious relaxation is immensely applicable to them.

3. Concentration

Practice focusing on just one thing at a time. Young people these days are constantly bombarded with external stimuli, be it on their devices, in the car, listening to the radio, watching TV, or the floods of information received at school. They are expected to multitask and take in a lot of particulars at once, so learning to focus on just one thing can be a relief to their active minds, and it is a skill that has wide-ranging positive effects.

4. Meditation

The actual meditative experience is possible for children ages eleven to eighteen. Active meditations work well for this age group, but they can also succeed in more passive, seated meditations. They have greater attention spans which allow them to practice for longer periods of time.

Children in this age group are generally eager to explore their cognition and think for themselves. During meditation, cue them to notice their thoughts and thinking patterns. (Scripting for this is provided in the lesson plans to follow.)

As they activate new cognitive pathways, encourage nonjudgmental self-inquiry and discovery. Young people tend to be self-conscious and concerned about what their peers think. You, as the guide, can help abate these tendencies by reminding them that mindfulness is a safe place to explore and evolve themselves free of judgment.

As the facilitator, provide ample pauses during the meditative experience. You can get out of the way and allow students time and space to be present with their own internal experiences of mind and body. This is where they can get in the zone and marinade in their own experiences.

5. Reflection

Allot time for discussing, sharing, or journaling about their meditative experiences. Students may be hesitant to share openly unless they feel very comfortable among their peers. If they are amenable, you can facilitate open discussion and ask critical questions like, "How did the exercise make you feel, and why?" and "How can we apply this?" They can make these higher-thinking connections. If group discussion proves fruitless, have them draw or journal. They can quietly reflect and assimilate these new feelings into their everyday lives.

The Power of Visualization

I recall a guided visualization exercise I led with a group of elementary school children. I led them to visualize their "happy place" and asked them to notice all the sights, sounds, scents, feelings, and tastes of this place. Then I asked, "Is anyone in your happy place with you?" Relaxing music with nature sounds was playing in the background.

Afterward, a new student who I'd only just met said that the music reminded her of a time when she went on a nature walk with her late grandmother. Her visualization brought back those memories and emotions. I asked her how it made her feel and she said, "A little sad… but also a little happy because those are good memories and I think she would want me to smile."

Guided visualization with peaceful music can unlock profound experiences. Sometimes, all it takes is creating a safe and comfortable environment and holding space for the children to share their experiences with you.

– Kelly

Lesson Plan #5

Lesson: "Clear Sky"

Time: 60 minutes
Age group: 11+ year olds

Goals: Relax the body and focus the mind. Cultivate metacognition and empathy.

Materials Needed:

Outdoor space, towels, blankets, or yoga mats to lie on, optional writing utensils and paper or notebook for reflective journaling

SEL Core Competencies:

- Self-Awareness
- Self-Management
- Social Awareness
- Relationship SKills

1. Energy Regulation

(With the students, go for a walk or jog around the area. If you can, be outside in the neighborhood, school grounds, or a park. Leave electronic devices behind, and encourage the students to look around and notice as many small unique details about their environment as they can.

Allow time for a cooldown stretch or some light yoga. Encourage everyone to go at their own pace and not worry about what others may be doing.)

2. Conscious Relaxation

Now that we've stirred up our energy a bit, let's release any excess energy that we don't need. First, let's try horse breath. Take a deep breath in through your nose, and breathe out through your mouth, letting your lips make a nice loud relaxed motorboat sound just like a horse does when it's tired. It may feel strange and silly at first, but that's ok. We'll do it a few times all together.

Now let's try lion's breath. We'll inhale through the nose, and exhale through the mouth, except this time, open your mouth wide like you're saying "HAAAA." Stick out your tongue and make a growling sound at the back of your throat. Bonus points if you cross your eyes while you roar!

Don't worry about what you look like. Everyone else is crossing their eyes, too, so they can't even see you. Let's roar it out a few times all together!

3. Concentration

Make yourself comfortable either sitting or lying down. Bring your focus to your feet, the feet that just did some great work for us, jogging/walking around. Feel your feet begin to relax, letting go of any tension from the toes all the way to the heels.

Now feel that relaxation travel up into the legs, softening the ankles, calves, shins, knees, up over the thighs, glutes, and hips, so that the legs feel heavy as they rest on the earth.

Next, focus on your midsection. If you notice any holding or gripping in the belly or low back areas, let them be free and relaxed. Feel your breath rising and falling with ease. Let that ease travel up over your chest and then down from your heart center out through your arms, hands, and fingers.

Next, feel your neck and shoulders soften and relax. Release your jaw. Allow your tongue to become still, your eyelids to become heavy, and your eyebrows and forehead to completely relax.

4. Meditation

Gently open your eyes and gaze up at the sky. Relax your eyes and allow your vision to blur. Notice any shapes, colors, or objects drifting through the sky.

After a few minutes, when you feel comfortable, you can close your eyes once again. Visualize your mind like a clear blue sky. Any clouds, planes, or birds that drift into your sky are like your own thoughts, feelings, or memories.

The clouds in the sky are always in motion, being blown about by wind, materializing, and dissolving at any moment. Airplanes fly across the sky—there one minute and gone the next. The same happens with our thoughts. Remember, you are not that bird or airplane flying through the sky. You are the person watching that object pass through the sky, just like you are not your thoughts or feelings but rather the person observing and experiencing your thoughts and feelings on a moment-to-moment basis.

For the next several minutes, lie back and watch from a distance as your thoughts drift in and out of your mind, always coming back to that clear blue sky.

5. Reflection

- How did your body feel during our physical exercise? How does it feel now after the body scan and meditation practice? Why do you think that is?

- What thoughts or feelings came up for you during the Clear Sky visualization?

- Did you find the Clear Sky exercise challenging? Easy? Why?

- How can you apply what we've practiced here to your everyday life?

Lesson Plan #6

Lesson: "Share Your Light"   Time: 60 minutes
Age group: 11+ year olds

Goals: Relax the body and focus the mind. Cultivate metacognition and empathy.

Materials Needed:

Writing utensils and paper or notebook for reflective journaling

SEL Core Competencies:

- Self-Awareness
- Self-Management
- Social Awareness
- Relationship Skills

1. Energy Regulation

(Lead the group through a yoga sun salutation warmup. You can preface this exercise by saying it was originally practiced in ancient times as a moving meditation done facing toward the rising or setting sun. Encourage the students to match their breath to each movement and follow at their own pace. If you are unfamiliar with sun salutation, you can search online videos for reference.)

- Inhale. Stretch your arms up overhead.
- Exhale. Fold forward and reach for your toes.
- Inhale. Halfway lift and look forward.
- Exhale. Bend the knees and plant the palms on the floor.
- Inhale. Step the feet back into a plank position. Option to lower the knees down.
- Exhale. Bend the elbows and lower down all the way onto the mat.
- Inhale. Place palms down on the mat beside each shoulder, then press through your hands to lift the chest for cobra pose.
- Exhale. Press up through tabletop, curl the toes under, lift the knees, and press back into downward dog.
- Inhale. Step or hop the feet up towards the hands.
- Exhale. Forward fold.
- Inhale. Press down through the feet to rise back up to standing with arms overhead.
- Exhale. Bring the palms together in front of the heart.
- Repeat this sequence three to five times.

2. Conscious Relaxation

Come to a comfortable seated or reclined position. Rest your hands on top of your legs or belly, and if it feels right, close your eyes. Notice the rhythm of your breathing after that bit of movement. Do you feel a sense of warmth or tingling anywhere throughout your body? Maybe you notice some perspiration?

Bring your focus to the muscles in your face: your eyebrows, eyes, cheeks, jaw, lips, and tongue. With your next breath, envision sending your breath to these areas, filling them up with the inhale, and on the exhale feel them relax, any tension or tightness melting away.

Now focus on your neck and shoulders. Send your next few breaths into this area of your body, feeling stress dissolve as you breathe out.

Next, bring your focus to your chest, arms, and hands. Inhale to fill up these areas with breath. Exhale to feel them become soft and heavy; no need to hold or grip anything here.

Move your focus to your midsection: the abdomen and lower back. Let go of any holding. Let the breath move easily in and out of these areas.

Focus now on your hips and pelvis. With your next exhale, release any gripping or holding here as well. Relax from the inside out.

Move your attention to your legs. These are some of our bodies' biggest and strongest muscles. One breath at a time, give these muscles permission to relax and let go. Feel the legs get heavier as your focus moves over the knees, calves, shins, and finally to the ankles and feet.

As you continue to breathe, if you notice any tension arise anywhere throughout your body, simply send a breath to that area, and relax and release on the exhale.

3. Concentration

Now concentrate on the area of your heart. Imagine the flickering flame of a candle sitting in the center of your heart. And with every breath, that flame grows a little brighter. It continues to grow brighter and brighter, growing into a glowing ball of light that emanates out from the center of your body, filling your head, arms, and legs. The light eventually grows bigger than your physical body and shines outward into the world.

4. Meditation

Next, visualize someone you love. As you breathe, imagine sending your light to the heart of your loved one. See the candle in their heart ignite. Watch their light grow. Your hearts are connected by this internal flame you've created. As it fills you and overflows from your body, it is shared with this other person until they are overflowing as well. Notice how it makes you feel to share your light with someone special. Imagine how they may feel receiving this light from you, wherever they are in the world right now.

5. Reflection

- How do your body and mind feel now compared to when we started?
- What thoughts or feelings came up for you during the exercise?
- What was your favorite part of the practice and why?
- How did you feel when you imagined light shining out of your heart? When you imagined sending that light to someone else?
- How can you apply what we just practiced to your everyday life?

12 Mindful Moments

Listed below are twelve quick and simple calming activities for any time and place: the back seat of the car, while getting ready for bed, seated at the dinner table, and so on. Designed with juggling parents, teachers, and caregivers in mind!

1. **Starfish Breath** – Extend one hand with the five fingers spread wide like a starfish. Using the pointer finger of your opposite hand, trace from the base of your thumb up and down each finger until you reach the base of the pinky. Then trace back again. When your finger traces upward, breathe in. When your finger traces downward, breathe out. Move slowly and evenly.

2. **Ocean Breath** – Place your hands over your ears and breathe in and out slowly through your nose. Imagine your breath is the sound of ocean waves ebbing and flowing. Focus on this sound for five to ten breaths.

3. **Butterfly Hug** – Wrap your arms around yourself so that your hands are resting on your opposite shoulders. Take deep breaths, feeling this nice warm hug, then begin to tap your shoulders gently with your hands, as though little butterflies have landed on your shoulders and are tapping hello.

4. **Four-Square Breath** – Use your finger to trace the shape of a square in the air. As you trace from one corner to the next, breathe in for a count of 1, 2, 3, 4. Pause at the corner and hold your breath for a count of 1, 2, 3, 4, then trace to the next corner and breathe out for a count of 1, 2, 3, 4. Hold your breath here for a count of 1, 2, 3, 4. Repeat this pattern from corner to corner of the square, as many times as needed to find calm.

5. **Squeeze and Release** – Clench your hands into fists. Squeeze tightly as you take a deep breath in, then as you exhale release your fists and let your hands be loose and floppy.

6. **Visiting Feelings** – When you're feeling a big emotion or sensation in your body, think of it like a visitor or guest in your home. It will be there for only a short while. It comes with a message. What message is this feeling trying to tell you? Take a few moments to sit with your visitor, listen to what it has to say, and then kindly say goodbye to it and be on your way.

7. **Bunny Rabbit Breath** – Like a bunny rabbit with a twitchy little nose, take several short sniffs in through your nose, then one big breath out your mouth like "Haaaa." Repeat this three to five times and notice how you feel.

8. **I Spy** – Pick a color, perhaps your favorite color, and look around. See how many places you can spot this color in the space around you. When you see this color, how does it make you feel?

9. **Bird Breath** – Breathe in and stretch your arms out and up like wings. Breathe out and lower them back down again. Continue this over and over as many times as you like. Maybe imagine yourself taking flight like a bird and soaring up into the air, looking down at the objects and people from a distance.

10. **Opposite Search** – Look around the space you are in and see if you can find things that are opposite of each other. Something old and something new. Something heavy and something light. Something white, something black. Something alive, something dead. Something hot and something cold. How creative can you be in your search? And how many tiny details can you notice about the world around you?

11. **Raindrops** – With your fingers, begin gently tapping the top of your head, like raindrops falling from the sky. Notice the feeling. Then play with the raindrops getting heavier and faster, and lighter and slower. Maybe the raindrops move down to your face, neck, and shoulders. How does it feel?

12. **Hot Hands** – Bring the palms of your hands together and rub them quickly, creating friction and heat between them. Rub faster and faster. After a few moments, separate your hands and notice the heat emanating from them. Place your hands over your eyes and feel their warmth relax your face. Place your hands over your shoulders and feel any tension relax. Place your hands over your belly and take a slow, deep breath.

9. Activity Guide

The chart below lists all activities in this book. It is your one-stop reference for quickly choosing age-appropriate activities and lesson plans according to your needs.

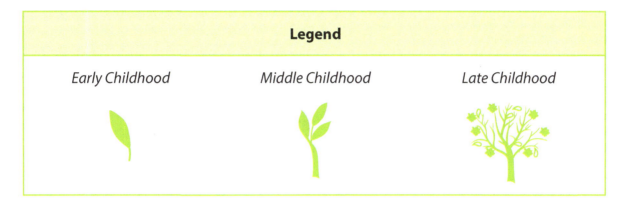

Legend		
Early Childhood	Middle Childhood	Late Childhood

Lesson / Activity	Pages	Age Groups
Feather Fun	24–25	
Thunderstorm	26–27	
Storm Starters	28	
Magic Musical Mats	31–33	
Glitter & Color	34–36	
Clear Sky	41–43	
Share Your Light	44–46	

Lesson / Activity	Pages	Age Groups
12 Mindful Moments	47–48	
Hand Model of the Brain	55–57	
Upstairs Downstairs Brain	58-61	
Sun of Awareness	62–65	
Academic Subjects	67–69	
Nine Intelligences	69–76	
Nervous System Soothers	82–83	

Conclusion

We hope these tips, strategies, and activities show you how fun it can be to guide children through meditation and mindfulness. We suggest doing the exercises yourself a few times to become familiar with them and develop your own verbiage. Make notes in the margins to add your ideas and things you might like to say during the exercises. Make them your own!

Part III

Extra Nutrients

The value of education is not the learning of many facts but the training of the mind to think.

–Albert Einstein

With a basic understanding of the brain, we begin to see why mindfulness works. This part of the book looks at contemporary models for understanding the brain, especially as they pertain to children's social, emotional, and cognitive development. These models provide basic underpinnings for the vast applications of meditation and mindfulness. They can serve as primers (taught in as few as five minutes), prior to a mindfulness activity.

Chapter 12 discusses how to incorporate mindfulness, meditation, and other emerging imperatives of *Social-Emotional Learning* (SEL) into modern academic curricula. All information here in Part Three can be adapted to your teaching domain, style, and interests, for instance the customizable approaches to mindfulness based on Howard Gardner's *Multiple Intelligences*, discussed in Chapter 13.

10. How the Brain Works

> Each time we discover something new about ourselves, we discover something new about existence, about the world around us.
>
> *–Sujantra*

The *mind*, as you may suspect, plays a central role in *mindfulness*. The many mysteries as well as the known powers of the human mind can supply those interested with endless avenues of exploration. Merriam-Webster's online dictionary defines *mind* as "the element or complex of elements in an individual that feels, perceives, thinks, wills, and especially reasons." The definition alone leaves plenty of room for exploration!

When teaching children about the mind, it helps to present it as—very simply—a tool. The mind is a vital tool in our toolboxes for creating and sustaining healthy, joyful lives. This tool can be a helping hand, a guiding light, and a trusted friend. What's more, the brain is proving to be pliable to our very relationship with it.

Recent research elucidates the idea that our neurons (brain cells) and neural pathways can physically alter, restructure, and rewire depending on our environment, our experiences, and our thoughts. In other words, neurons are responsive to what we learn, perceive, and experience, and they will organize and reorganize themselves accordingly. This process is referred to as *neuroplasticity*.[1]

Parts of the Brain

AMYGDALA
"Mammal Brain"
"Emotional Brain"
"Downstairs Brain"

PREFONTAL CORTEX
"Human Brain"
"Thinking Brain"
"Upstairs Brain"

BRAIN STEM
"Lizard Brain"
"Survival Instincts Brain"
"Downstairs Brain"

When it comes to mindfulness and meditation, evidence from neuroscience and brain imaging continues to shed light on their ability to profoundly and reliably alter the form and function of the brain to improve a person's quality of both thought and feeling.[2]

Equipped with these science-backed insights, you can be confident in guiding children to explore the wonderful nature of their minds and the myriad ways they can use their minds to keep life fun, positive, fulfilling, and meaningful.

Let's look at a few representational models of the brain and mind. These can be adapted to different age groups and taught as brief primers to mindfulness and meditation experiences.

Hand Model of the Brain

One key representational model effective with children of all ages is the *Hand Model of the Brain*, developed by neuroscientist, psychiatrist, and professor Dr. Dan Siegel. By forming your hand into a fist, with your thumb curled and tucked between your palm and fingers, the fist comes to represent the brain. The front of the brain is where the fingers curl around, and this represents the space behind the forehead, called the prefrontal cortex. This is the part of the brain that is the last to become fully formed, around age twenty-five. It is also the most highly evolved part of the brain, present only in humans and select great apes. The prefrontal cortex is our center for logic, reason, critical thinking, problem solving, and higher learning.

When you unfold the fingers and look at the center of the brain where your thumb is folded in, we find the amygdala, a major component of the limbic brain. This central region of the brain attaches to the back of the frontal lobe and is the storehouse of our emotional memories.

When we are young and learning about the world, this part of the brain learns to recognize our emotional experiences as either "good" or "bad" to protect us for the future. For example, if, as a young child, a dog barked at you and you became afraid, the limbic brain would store the experience and the association of fear with dogs barking. So, as an adult, you may hear a dog bark or see a big dog and immediately feel fright and either freeze or stay away. This is your brain's attempt to protect you and increase your chances of survival. In sum, the limbic brain (here depicted as the thumb) perceives potential threats and communicates them via emotion.

Now, your wrist, or the base of your brain, also known as the brain stem, is where your spinal cord connects to your brain. This is the oldest part of the human brain, evolutionarily speaking, and all vertebrates have it, including reptiles. Therefore, it is sometimes referred to as the "lizard brain." This part of our brain regulates involuntary bodily functions: things like breathing, digestion, body temperature, pupil dilation, and the heartbeat. We do not have to think about any of these things for them to happen in our bodies. They happen automatically.

Hand Model of the Brain

PREFRONTAL CORTEX

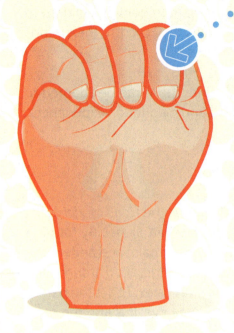

1

When the prefrontal cortex, amygdala, and brain stem are working together harmoniously, we are able to process our thoughts and feelings using logic and reason. We can think creatively and solve problems as they arise.

2

When we perceive a threat, real or imagined, the amygdala sends signals to the brain stem to activate our body's "fight, flight, freeze, or fawn" response. This overrides our "thinking brain" and impairs our ability to think logically and respond rationally to the situation. This is called "flipping our lid."

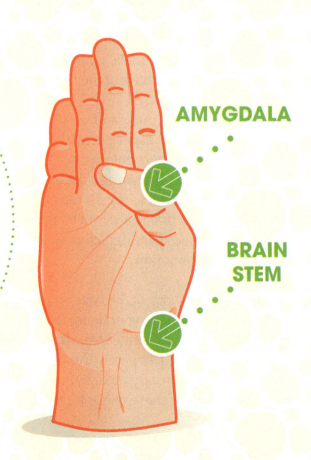

AMYGDALA

BRAIN STEM

The brain stem also communicates closely with the limbic brain and activates the autonomic nervous system, which is responsible for turning on fight-flight-freeze-fawn responses. When the limbic brain perceives a threat, it communicates the threat to the brain stem, which then switches the autonomic nervous system to hyperactive mode.

When we encounter a trigger that activates a strong emotion in the limbic brain, our brain stem can signal a warning to the body that it is in danger. In the heat of the moment, it is difficult for the prefrontal cortex—the front of the brain and center of logic—to know if we are or are not in actual physical danger. The prefrontal cortex struggles to function, because the brain has been hijacked by the limbic brain in an emotional response, and we have "flipped our lid."

With our hand, we can demonstrate the mechanics of this moment to a child. With the hand curled together in the shape of a fist, thumb tucked in, it represents a brain that is functioning harmoniously and coherently. Then, by popping open the fingers like the lid of a can, we have flipped our lid, i.e., the part of our brain that manages logic, reason, and deliberate thinking has gone offline. We are in a state of emotional response.

Interestingly, the chemical response in the brain that triggers the emotional reaction lasts in the body for only about ninety seconds. That said, we often stay in an emotion for much longer than ninety seconds because of the thought patterns that continuously re-trigger the limbic brain.

For example, when we see a dog and it triggers the emotional memory of the fear of dogs that is stored in our limbic brain, the limbic brain communicates to the brain stem that we are in danger. In response, our heartrate increases to pump blood more quickly. Blood flows to the extremities and away from the digestive system so that we can mobilize our limbs to sprint for our lives. The pupils of our eyes dilate to take in more of our surroundings. Our breath rate increases to oxygenate our muscles to prepare for the fight for our life. Thus, the physiological stress response begins.

At this point, our lid is flipped. Our brain is hampered from communicating to itself that "It's just a dog! You're not in actual danger. It's okay. You're safe." In the throes of this emotional response, the brain cannot logically compute that it is safe, and everything is fine.

By sharing with children the techniques to calm and ground themselves, they will eventually become masters at managing their own stress responses. By learning how to bring their prefrontal cortices back online, they will be able to self-regulate and avoid negative behaviors when they do become emotional. Because children's brains are still developing, it is all the more impactful for them to wire these methods of self-regulation into their powerhouses while they are young. Children can learn that although feelings and emotions are natural and inevitable, there are tools for self-soothing and preventing their feelings from taking over completely.

MY UPSTAIRS AND DOWNSTAIRS BRAIN

My upstairs brain helps me to:

- think before I act
- make thoughtful decisions
- maintain awareness of my emotions and body
- stay focused and centered
- be empathetic toward others.

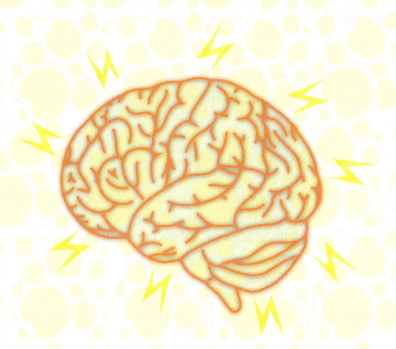

My downstairs brain:

- activates my fight, flight, freeze, and fawn responses
- ignites my emotions
- controls unconscious bodily functions
- allows me to move and act instinctively.

Upstairs Downstairs Brain

Another helpful model for understanding the mind, also conceived by Dr. Siegel, is the *Upstairs Downstairs Brain.* This model helps young people to visualize their thoughts and feelings as a two-story house where their reasoning and higher thinking live upstairs, and their baser instincts and emotions live downstairs. The basic outline of a house (a vertical rectangle with a triangle roof on top) can be replicated easily by most young children through a fun drawing and coloring exercise.

We can talk with them about how the house represents the brain. By dividing the house in half, we have an upstairs brain and a downstairs brain. The downstairs brain is where big emotions are activated. This part of the house lights up when something makes them angry, scared, nervous, or sad. This area is also where emotional memories live. For example, the time they saw a big, scary dog that was barking loudly.

Encourage the children to talk about what happens in their bodies, physically, when they are experiencing that big emotion. "When I'm angry, my face turns red, and I clench my fists." "When I'm scared, I get knots in my stomach, and I start to sweat." These are images we can help them draw or help them communicate when talking about the downstairs brain.

The upstairs brain represents the prefrontal cortex. This part of the house is where our planning, thinking, imagining, and reasoning abilities reside. Happy memories are stored here, as well. Here, we can offer comforting images of mom giving me a hug, grandpa bringing me a gift, or of playing outside with my friends. Maybe there's a hobby or talent I possess that brings me to a state of creative flow. These images and activities generate positive, constructive emotions in the brain and allow us to behave as our best selves.

After establishing an understanding of the upstairs-downstairs model of the brain, it's important to emphasize the way the two stories of the house connect and can enhance one another. The downstairs, "lizard" brain powers our big emotions and is full of energy, enthusiasm, excitement, and our fight-flight-freeze-fawn responses, while our upstairs brain powers our higher thinking, ability to make controlled decisions, and imagination. By learning to *channel* the diverse energies of our upstairs and downstairs brains, we can create our lives with personal intention and self-mastery.

Thus, the staircase of the house takes on a significant role. You can explain to the children, "Imagine if you were stuck in your downstairs brain all the time. You're full of the energy and excitement fueled by the downstairs brain, but you can't figure out what to do with it." Or, "You're upset with someone, but you can't sort it out because you can't access the higher-order problem solving of the upstairs brain." Here, the stairway is a powerful link that can be strengthened through mindfulness and meditation. The many methods provided in this book become ways of traveling between the two stories of the metaphorical house.

Another impactful realization for children is that the downstairs brain controls bodily functions. Oftentimes, poorly controlled bodily functions become a source of embarrassment for children. The solution here is to draw upon the self-control center of the upstairs brain, where conscious and deliberate movements of the body and emotions can be cultivated.

Foster conversation and let the children know it is natural for our brains to become cluttered, busy, or challenged. Occasionally, if we are caught in an emotion, the stairway from our downstairs brain to our upstairs brain may be blocked. The good news is that we can prepare for these instances. Prompt the students to identify which healthy coping mechanisms or calming exercises they could use to transition from the downstairs brain to the upstairs brain.

Say, for example, the child gets into a fight with a sibling and becomes profusely angry. The child's downstairs brain has been activated, and he or she needs to find a route to the upstairs brain to access calmer thinking. You can remind the child of a few techniques covered earlier in this book, and perhaps the child identifies the Starfish Breath as an effective way to calm down.

The next time a conflict arises, the child—instead of picking a fight, running away, clamming up in a freeze response, or surrendering to a disempowered fawn response—can slow the momentum of the situation by pausing for a few deep starfish breaths. The child can then return to the situation from the vantage of a calm, peaceful upstairs brain. The child may even be able to open a line of communication with his is or her sibling to discuss a level-headed solution to the conflict.

The ability, through practice, to move consciously between biochemical responses (i.e., "parts" of the brain) is an invaluable life skill that can positively influence the trajectory of children's lives.

Inside my Mind

Imagine that your mind is a two-story house made up of your upstairs brain and your downstairs brain. Draw pictures, symbols, colors, or words to show what goes on in your upstairs brain and your downstairs brain. On the staircase, write down your favorite calming exercises that help you move back to your upstairs brain from your downstairs brain.

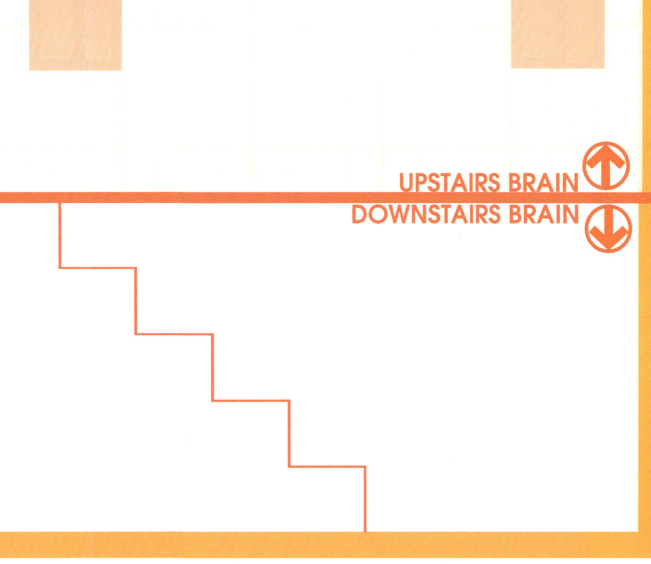

UPSTAIRS BRAIN ⬆

DOWNSTAIRS BRAIN ⬇

EXTERNAL
SENSATIONS

FEELINGS

C
A
U
S
A
T
I
O
N

FEELINGS ABOUT OURSELVES

BODY
SENSATIONS

SELF-ESTEEM

MEMORIES

EGO

WORLD

TIME

SELF

SPACE

SELF-TALK

ME
MINE

I AM
SUBJECTIVE
AWARENESS

DUALITY

THOUGHTS

IMAGES

DREAMS

THE SUN OF AWARENESS

EXPLORE YOUR MIND!

The core of the sun is the subjective sense of Self,
our foundational feeling of being: I am. As children we emerge from
this unconscious state through bodily sensations and create our
dualistic view of reality: ego and sense of other.

The enduring feeling surrounding ego is self-esteem, how we feel
about ourselves, thoughts, emotions, and actions. A healthy ego
and self-esteem emerge from environments of love, wisdom,
and learning.

On the outside edge of the sun are the components by which
we construct our detailed sense of the world: sensations, self-talk,
images, thoughts, imagination, memories, feelings, and dreams.

The three rays of the sun which tie together the fabric of mind are
space, time, and causation. All of the challenges, joys, and sufferings
that we encounter in life can be conceptualized through
the sun of awareness.

SUN OF AWARENESS

Write your name in the center of the sun. This is your inner place of knowing, your sense of "I" or "me." Now take a moment to close your eyes and become aware of three body sensations, three mental images, three thoughts, and three emotions or feelings that you are experiencing right now. Write these things down in the space along the rays of the Sun.

SENSATIONS

IMAGES

FEELINGS

THOUGHTS

Finally, look at your Sun of Awareness and feel your sense of self as the observer of all that is going on around and inside you.

Sun of Awareness

As we mature, we begin to think abstractly. Mathematics, philosophy, ethics, psychology, empathy, and a range of other subjects require and help to deepen abstract thinking. Many of us will also develop the ability to ponder our own thoughts and mental habits, a process called *metacognition*, which has been mentioned in various parts of this book.

Students can explore their cognition—and thereby practice metacognition—using the *Sun of Awareness* diagram, adapted from Dr. Seigel's concept of the *Wheel of Awareness*. The Sun of Awareness helps to shed light on our consciousness and all the challenges, joys, and experiences we naturally encounter in life.

In the diagram, the center of the sun represents the subjective awareness of the self: one's fundamental feeling of being. It can be equated with the thought "I am." Children develop this state unconsciously. Through meditative and mindful practices, we seek to reconnect consciously with this dimension of ourselves, to gain a deeper awareness of who we are.

As young children become conscious of external environments and bodily sensations, they develop an awareness of both the outer world and a concept of themselves within the world. At this point, the ego and a dualistic sense of oneself in the world emerge from the self. In other words, the child begins to see herself, her ego, as separate from the world she lives in.

The enduring feeling surrounding ego is self-esteem: how we feel about ourselves, our thoughts, emotions, and actions. A healthy ego and positive sense of self-esteem emerge from environments of love, wisdom, and learning. A child with healthy self-esteem is aware of the inner resources that help him or her interface positively and constructively with the world. A wellspring of self-worth, self-acceptance, and self-confidence is felt within the child.

On the outer edge of the sun are the components we use to construct our sense of the world: bodily sensations, external sensations, self-talk, thoughts, memories, feelings, and dreams. Finally, the rays of the sun that tie together the fabric of the mind are the concepts of space, time, and causation (cause and effect).

Healthy individuals are aware of all rays of their "sun" and recognize the need for balance among the varying elements. A healthy ego and self-esteem can be maintained when they see themselves through a holistic, integrated lens. They regard the full range of their thoughts, feelings, and behaviors with compassion, acceptance, self-love, and good humor. When mistakes are made or bad moods blow in, they can realize—with tenderness—that they are human!

Furthermore, well-balanced individuals hold personalized worldviews while acknowledging that the views of others, even if different from their own, are also valid. Imbalance occurs when we do not think well of ourselves, we fixate on unhelpful thoughts or feelings, and we think our ideas and perceptions are the only valid perspective.

Meditation and mindfulness can help children strengthen their cognitive abilities, but more importantly, meditation and mindfulness give children time and space to observe and reflect on who they are at the core, without imprints, labels, and expectations from the outside world contaminating their deeper sense of self.

11. Social and Emotional Learning

Through meditation, we explore a depth of awareness concerning ourselves, our lives, and the world that would otherwise rarely be accessed. The daily practice of meditation allows us time for self-reflection and contemplation.

–Sujantra

Mindfulness is more than a handful of feel-good activities to do when under stress. Woven into daily practice and lifestyle, it facilitates deeper self-understanding, enhances cognitive ability, boosts vitality and levels of contentment, reinforces healthy coping mechanisms, and improves academic and work performance. Mindfulness helps us find more than a few moments of temporary calm. It helps us grow into full, self-embodied human beings who are equipped with essential life skills.

While young people learn their multiplication tables and grammar in school, they are often expected to already know how to sit still, pay attention, play nicely, get along with their peers, and how to express strong emotions without throwing a fit. The truth (and teachers know it all too well) is that many children come to school without these skills. While students with behavioral challenges sometimes receive help from school specialists, there has not been a catch-all course in school that teaches social, emotional, and behavioral health.

Enter the era of *Social-Emotional Learning* (SEL). Social-emotional learning is the terminology used within the current educational paradigm to describe the process by which young people learn how to understand themselves, manage their thoughts and emotions, and form positive relationships with others. Needless to say, SEL is foundational to healthy human development.

A growing body of research shows that SEL is also fundamental to academic success. The empirical evidence behind this concept is prompting educators to consider how they might integrate this type of learning into everyday instruction. While teachers know instinctively that SEL is important, schools have been focused primarily on teaching traditional academic content such as reading, math, science, and history, and have been less intentional about fostering the social and emotional skills that are so important to learning and life success.

The concept of social-emotional learning, however, is gaining steam. As of this writing, SEL is required curriculum in thirty of the United States. According to California's Department of Education website, "Social and emotional learning reflects the critical role of positive relationships and emotional connections in the learning process and helps students develop a range of skills they need for school and life."[1]

The five core competencies of SEL are as follows.

- **Self-awareness**: the ability to recognize one's thoughts, emotions, and values.

- **Self-management**: the skill of managing one's emotions and behaviors to achieve one's goals.

- **Social awareness**: the ability to show empathy and consideration for others.

- **Relationship skills**: the abilities to form positive relationships, work collaboratively, and effectively navigate conflict.

- **Responsible decision making**: the ability to make constructive and appropriate choices about one's personal and social behavior.

Helping young people (and ourselves) to develop and utilize these skills makes for more pleasant home and learning environments and a better quality of life. But how exactly do we go about teaching these things?

Conveniently, the core competencies of SEL are closely aligned with the highly documented benefits of meditation and mindfulness. If SEL is the goal, then mindfulness is the method by which we can achieve it. Educators need tools to meet the rapidly growing demand for SEL, and the exercises, lesson plans, and theories presented in this book speak directly to that need.

For parents and caregivers at home, using these practices to nurture the social and emotional development of your children complements the learning happening in schools. It also nurtures a loving home environment where positive relationships abound, feelings are safely expressed, and each person within the family unit has a respectful regard for oneself and each other.

By pragmatically weaving the principles of mindfulness and meditation into both educational and home environments, we become part of the vital shift toward a culture of individuals who know how to identify and regulate emotions, treat themselves and others with empathy and respect, and design healthy and happy futures through the powers of intention and focus.

12. Mindfulness at School

While the demands imposed by school systems can make mindfulness seem like a luxury teachers cannot accommodate, the reality is, most schools cannot afford to function without it. Educators who practice mindfulness themselves are better equipped to navigate student behavioral issues, challenging peer and family dynamics, and overall workloads. Mindfulness alone can reduce teacher burnout and absenteeism.

Adding to that, mindfulness in schools has a measured impact on student behavior, learning outcomes, and overall well-being. While strict academic guidelines and busy schedules do not leave a lot of room for meditation and mindfulness during the school day, students can learn to use their mental and emotional capacities in new and exciting ways while staying within existing curriculum bounds.

Teachers who sprinkle even a few of the seeds we discuss below will notice a positive shift in classroom culture. Students who are restless or bored with the incessant demands of schooling may perk up when prompted to take three rounds of breath with their classmates. Students who are prone to bully others and engage in high-risk behaviors may learn to harmonize (quite literally) and cooperate with their peers through a group "hum."

Even when an activity fails to reach every student, the phenomenon of *emotional contagion* can positively influence a classroom if even one student finds calm in a meditation. The calm of one person can spread to others, creating a ripple effect of collective calm.

Here we offer suggestions for how to fertilize traditional academic subjects with mindfulness. These techniques can boost focus, brighten the imagination, heighten abstract thinking, expand empathetic awareness, and engender a greater capacity for self-reflection and insight—all skills which can improve scholastic performance and overall quality of life.

Science

- When studying the principles of nature, have students visualize a principle in action, and then have them imagine that same force operating in their own minds and bodies. For example, the continuous cycle of day and night: sometimes we are full of energy (daytime), and other times we grow quiet and need reflection (evening). Nature is in a constant state of change, and so are our bodies and minds. These changes are natural and healthy.

- Einstein used thought experiments to derive basic principles in his Theory of Relativity. Allow children time to use their imaginations to visualize a comet's orbit or the movement of an asteroid belt. Prompt them to feel the pull of gravity on their bodies.

- When teaching about the nervous system, include science-based figures that back the meditation experience. See Chapter 14 for help with this!

Math

- Encourage students to visualize numbers or see multiplication in their minds. They can also imagine numbers as animals or objects. One is a candle, two is a swan, and so on. Allow numbers to become an enjoyable part of thinking and not something to be feared.

- Link geometry to cubist paintings, or link division to the frets on a guitar. Explore how dividing a guitar string in half changes the pitch. Hum along with the various notes.

Language Arts

- Encourage closed eyes and imaginative listening to well-written literature. This allows children to feel the scenes and characters in a personal way.

- Explore the meaningful sounds of poetry. *Prosody*, a term referring to the patterns of rhythm and sound in language, is known to prompt relaxation in the nervous system.

- Play with letters in the mind's eye. For example, anagrams… Listen = silent.

- Offer and allow visualization in class. For example, encourage empathy toward people of the past. What might the students have done if confronted with x, y, z situation in history?

Giving children a way to explore their bodies, thoughts, moods, and emotions is invaluable to their education and personal growth. Meditation and mindfulness activities can show them how much agency they have over these aspects of themselves. There is perhaps no better time or place than the school setting to introduce children to these approaches to well-being.

13. The Nine Intelligences

Each of us experiences life in a unique way, and each of us brings our unique capacities to the world. People often think of intelligence as represented by one's score on a psychometric test, such as an Intelligence Quotient (IQ) test or the Scholastic Aptitude Test (SAT), but contemporary research points to an alternative concept: that these conventional measurements of intelligence often fail to reveal the nuances of an individual's particular strengths and weaknesses. The lyrical genius of Joni Mitchell, for example, could not be measured by such tests, nor could the visual capacities of Pablo Picasso.

The notion of human intelligence is thus shifting away from the concept of a singular, holistic capacity and more toward the recognition of multiple, diverse aptitudes possessed in varying degrees by different individuals. One such philosophy emerged with Howard Gardner's seminal work, *Frames of Mind: The Theory of Multiple Intelligences*.[1] Gardner proposed that intelligence does not manifest in any one way, but that each person has multiple intelligences, each varying in degree of facility.

Within you and within everyone are the seeds of each of Gardner's proposed Nine Intelligences, and yet, each of us is drawn to one or two of the intelligences more than the others. Furthermore, at various times in our lives, we may be keen to engage different aptitudes. When working with very young children, keep in mind that a few of the intelligences have not yet come online but may begin to show in middle and late childhood.

THE TYPES OF INTELLIGENCE

SPATIAL
Visualizing the world in three dimensions

NATURALIST
Understanding nature and living things

MUSICAL
Discerning sounds, their pitch, tone, rhythm, and timbre

LOGICAL-MATHEMATICAL
quantifying things, making hypotheses and proving them

EXISTENTIAL
tackling the questions of why we live and why we die

INTERPERSONAL
sensing people's feelings and motives

BODILY-KINESTHETIC
coordinating your mind with your body

LINGUISTIC
finding the right words to express what you mean

INTRAPERSONAL
understanding yourself, what you feel, and what you want

This chapter looks at how we can tailor mindfulness experiences to a person's unique capacities *and* help them explore their lesser-developed intelligences. Familiarity with this concept will engender inclusivity in your teaching style. You will begin to recognize how each child best identifies with his or her surroundings. One child may consistently nurture the plant on the windowsill (naturalist) while another may regularly build new structures with Legos (spatial). You can create experiences that empower students to draw upon their innate strengths *and* challenge them to engage their weaker areas with curiosity and non-judgment.

Mindfulness Exercises for the Nine Intelligences

Spatial Intelligence

Ability to visualize the world in 3D.

Discover Details

During guided visualizations, guide students to develop spatial awareness by cueing them to inspect their imagined spaces and notice as many details as possible. Include the five senses. What do they see? Hear? Smell? What might they be able to reach out and feel? Is there anything they can taste? How do the sensory details work together to create the whole scene?

Body-Space Awareness

Create body-space awareness by warming up with yoga postures, which can include partner yoga poses.

Naturalist Intelligence

Ability to understand living things and natural phenomena.

Scavenger Hunt

Go on a scavenger hunt in nature and prompt the children to notice details as they move around. "Do you see a snail shell? A yellow leaf? Do you hear the wind? What does this sideways-growing tree mean?" Guide them to an awareness of the present moment.

Flower Breath

Use the image of a flower to teach a breathing exercise. "*Breathe in* as if you are smelling a flower. *Breathe out* like you are gently blowing on the flower's petals."

Musical Intelligence

Ability to discern sounds, their pitch, tone, rhythm, and timbre.

Listen and Identify
Listen to music and ask the children if they can identify different instruments in the song, a male or female voice, dynamics such as louder or softer, and so on. Have them choose one instrument and conjure up a color, an emotion, or a scene from nature that they associate with that musical sound.

Play an Instrument
If you or the child play an instrument, you can play notes, chords, or a melody that express something—maybe the melody tells a story, expresses a feeling, or paints a picture. Discuss one or two of the many meanings music can create.

Sing or Hum
Guide the children to sing or hum their exhalations. Take a deep inhalation and then sing or hum a note or vowel in unison on the exhale. This exercise naturally elongates exhalation, which calms the nervous system.

Bell or Gong
Ring a bell or gong to practice active listening. Have the children raise their hands when they perceive that the tone of the bell or gong has finally ended.

The Young Musician

A young girl in my neighborhood likes to stop by and watch my friends and me play music on the lawn. One day, she brought a harmonica with her. She was experimenting with playing it, cueing off my friend who plays blues harmonica. It appeared to me that she was eager to develop her musical intelligence.

We started playing a game to help her express herself through music. I would make a statement and she would give a musical response. The game involved her relationship with her mom. I would say, "Paris, this is your mother, time to come in and do your homework." She would then create a sound on the harmonica. Then, "Paris, it's time to walk the dog… eat your broccoli, get up and go to school, be nice to your brother…"

Through the music, she was able to express her emotions about not only different activities in her life but also her relationship with her mother.

– *Sujantra*

Logical-Mathematical Intelligence

Ability to quantify things, make a hypothesis, run an experiment, and understand cause and effect.

Numbers and mathematics are an important part of modern living. Many adults are not comfortable with numbers. They become nervous when doing math and are not able to think mathematically regarding certain aspects of life that would benefit them, such as creating a personal budget.

When working with children, approaching math through a mindful lens can help even the most math-shy children become comfortable (and maybe even have fun!) with numbers.

Symbolic Math
Play games where numbers are linked to colors, images, or sounds. This helps children ease out of rigid "math-brain" thinking. For example, the equation 2+2=4 can be expressed by symbols other than numbers; the twos swans and the four a sailboat.

Breath Counting
Combine relaxation and math by counting the breath. Breathe in for a count of 1-2-3-4, and then breathe out for a count of 4-3-2-1. (See Four-Square Breath in Part Two under *Twelve Mindful Moments*.)

Logical Reflection
Ask critical-thinking and reflective questions after a meditation experience. These discussions help the children make conscious, logical connections between what they are practicing and how they feel. This engages their understanding of cause and effect. "When I breathe slowly, I feel calm. When I breathe quickly, I feel agitated," and so on.

Existential Intelligence

Ability to grapple with and tackle the big questions of why we live. What is our purpose here? What happens after we die?

Sun of Awareness

Use the *Sun of Awareness* diagram to engage children in a discussion about the various aspects of existence and their cognitive capacities. Help them conceptualize the interconnectedness of their sensations, thoughts, emotions, and behaviors. With practice and mindfulness, they can learn to manage themselves amid these various aspects of existence, and from them create meaningful lives.

Metacognition

With older children, practice metacognition by calling attention to thoughts, thought patterns, and associated moods. During reflection, ask students to either share verbally or write down what they found themselves thinking about during the meditation: grandma's declining health, a soccer game they played recently, an upcoming math test, all three? Let them know that by noticing their thoughts, they become present to their mental landscapes and therefore better able to direct and redirect thoughts as desired.

Interpersonal Intelligence

Ability to sense fellow humans' feelings and understand their motives.

Loving Kindness Meditation

Cultivate a feeling of love in your heart, such as a soft glowing light. Then visualize someone you love, and imagine sending that love to the person. Perhaps the soft light envelopes the person in an imaginary embrace.

Practice Empathy

Repeat an affirmation such as, "Just like me." This affirmation involves drawing to mind a person who is difficult to love or get along with. With that person in mind, think the words, "Just like me, this person is doing his or her best." "Just like me, this person sometimes feels insecure." "Just like me, this person has fears." "Just like me, this person has imperfections." "Just like me, this person needs love and kindness."

Bodily-Kinesthetic Intelligence

Ability to coordinate one's mind with one's body.

Becoming grounded and conscious in our bodies is an enormous part of childhood. We experience life and express ourselves through our bodies in ways we cannot do through thinking. Children are constantly responding with their bodies to commands made by adults and society: "Get up for school, eat your breakfast, come here, do this, don't do that, stop running around." Use mindfulness and meditation to help children find joy and expression through their bodies.

Walking Meditation
Take the children on a walking meditation. As they move their bodies, have them pay attention to each step and detail of their physical movement.

Energy Regulation
The first of the *Five Mindfulness Stepping Stones* (i.e., energy regulation) is perfectly conducive to helping children experience their physicality with mindfulness. This can include yoga, dance, and stretching. See the lesson plans for energy-regulation exercises.

Linguistic Intelligence

Ability to find the right words to express what one means.

Reflection
The fifth of the *Five Mindfulness Stepping Stones* (i.e., reflection) is great for stimulating linguistic intelligence. After a meditation, ask questions and foster discussion. Have students verbalize what they felt and experienced. Prompt them to name three descriptive words to describe their post-meditative state. For children who know how to write, prompt them to capture their reflections in a personal journal. Encourage them to get creative with their descriptions, perhaps drafting a story.

Read Poetry
The cadence of poetry can calm and uplift one's mood. Read poetry to children or have them read aloud. Emphasize the meaningful effects of sound, rhythm, and vocal emphases. A classic example is the concept of onomatopoeia, whereby the sound of a word mimics the thing it is referring to, such as the *tick tock* of a clock.

Combine movement with poetry. Jump rope games, for example, can represent the metrics of song and poetry.

Intrapersonal Intelligence

Ability to be in tune with one's own feelings, values, beliefs, and thinking processes.

Cultivate self-awareness among your students by helping them recognize their various bodily sensations, emotions, and thoughts. The *Sun of Awareness* diagram can serve as footing for this discussion. For example, prompt them to describe any differences they notice between thinking a thought and feeling an emotion. How do these states vary? Does one lead to the other? The *Storm Starters* worksheet can be used to pair emotional triggers with self-soothing techniques.

Inner Exploration

Identify an activity for each intelligence type that allows children to independently connect with their inner states. If a child is in a "mood" and you want to help them find direction in exploring that mood, have them scan through designated activities and select one that appeals to them. This gives the child autonomy in exploring his or her inner climate, which in turn facilitates self-discovery.

Examples:

- Visual-Spatial. What color are you feeling? Can you draw something with that color?

- Naturalist. Which animal sound would your feeling create? Which tree branch does your mind feel like right now?

- Bodily-Kinesthetic. Which walking style is your mood?

You will be amazed at how children can express themselves.

14. Stress and Its Antidote

When learning meditation and mindfulness, it helps to have a basic understanding of our bodies and how they navigate stress. We know that meditation and mindfulness are instrumental in mitigating and even preventing stress, but it helps to first understand the nature of stress and how our bodies strive to be the first line of defense against it.

The information in this chapter is more than enough to share with children, but it may inspire you to springboard further into research about stress, the nervous system, and their relevancy to mindfulness and meditation, which will in turn influence your personal approach to teaching the topics.

The Body's Stress Response

Mammals first appeared roughly 175 million years ago, primates 65 million years ago, and early humans seven million years ago. It is estimated that Homo sapiens, our modern human species, first appeared 200,000 years ago.

Far back in history, we humans battled for our lives against giant birds, crocodiles, leopards, grizzly bears, saber-toothed tigers, snakes, hyenas, Komodo dragons, and great apes. The human bodies we now inhabit are templated in an ancient biological system that evolved out of our efforts to survive. As a result, our nervous systems are highly responsive to stress.

According to KidsHealth website, stress is a function of the demands placed upon us and our ability to meet them. Today, these demands come not from protecting ourselves against wild animals but from societal factors such as family, jobs, friends, and school. Further demands arise from within each of us, often related to what we think we should be doing versus what we are able or willing to do.[1]

Advancements in modern technology impose another set of demands. Our engagement with mass media—the 24-hour news cycle, television, the internet, social media—engenders a feeling of *always on*. This constant activity is often the forerunner of diseases rooted in stress. Unfortunately, while the prevailing culture of our times has plenty of stressors, it does not prioritize relaxing and unwinding from that stress.

Our nervous systems respond to all forms of stress, whether mental, physical, real, or imagined. Stressful situations—whether time-bound, such as looming work deadlines and traffic jams, or chronic, such as persistent worry about social standing or financial difficulties—can trigger cascades of stress hormones. Over time, repeated activation of the stress response takes a toll on our physical and psychological health.

Even low-level stress, if chronic, keeps the body's stress response activated, much like a motor that idles when it should be turned off. Research shows that this type of stress contributes to high blood pressure, promotes the formation of artery-clogging deposits, and causes brain changes that may contribute to anxiety, depression, addiction, and obesity.[2]

Understanding The Nervous System

The activity of our bodies is regulated, both consciously and unconsciously, by the nervous system. The two main parts of the nervous system are the central nervous system, which is composed of the brain and spinal cord, and the peripheral nervous system, which is composed of the nerves that connect the central nervous system to the other parts of the body.

We will focus on the peripheral nervous system, because it houses a subsystem that is highly relevant to the study of mindfulness, namely the *autonomic nervous system*.

The autonomic nervous system controls processes that are unconscious, or involuntary. One branch of the autonomic nervous system is the *sympathetic* nervous system, which controls our fight, flight, freeze, and fawn responses. The other branch is the *parasympathetic* nervous system, which controls our rest and digest responses.

Understanding the dynamics of the sympathetic and parasympathetic nervous systems is key to navigating the body's stress response. With this knowledge, we begin to see how mindfulness plays a powerful role in keeping us in balance.

Evolutionarily, our two basic modes of existing are activity and rest. Activity mode includes the fight, flight, freeze, and fawn responses of the sympathetic nervous system. Rest mode includes digestion, repose, and sleep, and it is modulated by the parasympathetic nervous system.

We react to physical and psychological threats by fighting, fleeing, freezing, or fawning. Humans as well as other animals exhibit these behaviors. Fighting, we know well. To flee is to leave the situation or environment to avoid further danger. To freeze is to avoid further conflict by ceasing to move or act. The armadillo rolls up into a motionless ball. Some animals, by freezing, become invisible to the aggressor. This also involves doing nothing and letting the situation evolve. To fawn is to use words and actions, such as flattering or appeasing the aggressor, to try to diffuse conflict.

Autonomic (Involuntary) Nervous System

SYMPATHETIC

Fight, Flight, Freeze, or Fawn

- Adrenals release adrenaline
- Heart rate increases
- Breathing quickens
- Pupils dilate
- Digestion halts
- Skin becomes flushed
- Muscles tense or tremble

PARASYMPATHETIC

Rest and Digest

- Endocrine system releases tissue-building hormones
- Heart rate and blood pressure decrease
- Bronchials constrict to slow breathing
- Pupils constrict
- Stomach and intestines stimulate digestive fluids

The primary concern for people of the modern, developed world is psychological stress. When danger is perceived, the sympathetic nervous system provides a burst of energy and tells the body to get ready for physical and mental activity. It causes the heart to beat harder and faster, and it opens the airways for easy breathing. It also temporarily stops digestion so the body can focus on immediate physical movement.

When the threat has passed, the parasympathetic nervous system takes over, works to restore homeostasis, and remains active during the body's recuperation period. This system tells the body it is OK to relax, refuel, and reset. It causes a decrease in heart rate, stimulates smooth muscle movement of the intestines, and activates the secretion of saliva, digestive juices, and tissue-building hormones.

You can see how these two systems work in alternation. Every stress moment needs an equal rest moment. If we do not have that balance, we lose our stability both physically and psychologically. If we do not properly disengage or recover from the stresses in our lives, then our nervous systems will struggle to maintain balance.

The autonomic nervous system has thus evolved as a survival mechanism, enabling us to react quickly to life-threatening situations (real or perceived) and then return to equilibrium once the threat is gone. This system regulates processes in the body that we usually do not notice or control consciously, such as heart rate and metabolism. Breathing and breath rate, too, are usually managed involuntarily, but we can choose to consciously control our breathing. *Enter the power of mindfulness.* Mindful control of our breath is a key method to preventing or easing a stress response.

Thousands of years of evolution have resulted in a finely tuned nervous system designed to keep us both safe and in balance. To be healthy, we must respect the natural workings of this system and find ways to nurture ease and equilibrium in our bodies. We cannot submit ourselves to constant stress and stimulation and expect to remain in good health. We need to rest and digest. Mindfulness helps with this rebalancing.

Childhood Stress

Children are not immune to stress. Childhood stress can be present in any setting that requires adaptation or change. Stress may be caused by positive changes, such as starting a new activity, but more often it is linked with difficult transitions such as pubescence, social dynamics, illness, or disturbances in family life.

Stress is a natural part of life, and it can be good in moderate amounts, such as when a child experiences stage fright before a performance. This type of stress can be the child's indication that he or she is venturing outside of his or her comfort zone, and thus the stressor can be seen as a positive side effect of pursuing one's interests. Excessive stress, on the other hand, can adversely affect the way a child thinks, feels, and acts.

Because children need time to learn how to respond to stress as they grow and develop, stressors that are easily managed by an adult may be challenging for a child. Even minor changes can impact a child's sense of safety and security.

Just like the stresses of adulthood, childhood stress causes the nervous system to become imbalanced. The rest-and-digest functions of the parasympathetic nervous system are not given the time, space, or appropriate conditions to reestablish internal harmony, or homeostasis.

Unfortunately, the stress and trauma experienced in childhood can have detrimental effects on a child's mental and physical health far into adulthood. Adults who suffered trauma and high stress in childhood experience higher rates of post-traumatic stress disorder (PTSD), depression, disruptive behaviors, suicidality, substance-use disorders, as well as common medical disorders such as cardiovascular disease, obesity, chronic pain syndromes, gastrointestinal disorders, and immune dysregulation.[3]

What this means is that every effort to lovingly guide children through stressful experiences is augmented by the fact that such nurturing is provided during one of the most critical and impressionable periods of life: childhood. The rippling impact of these efforts cannot be overstated.

By approaching childhood stress holistically and with compassion, we as parents, educators, and caregivers can often identify the root causes of stress and work with children to lessen both the causes and effects of that stress. Even when we are unable to identify the root cause, we can still lovingly guide children along avenues of healthy stress management.

The foremost way to influence a child's relationship to stress is by being a positive role model. This means practicing the mindfulness you preach. Children learn by example, and it happens as naturally as osmosis. Don't expect yourself to be perfect; just know that in your openness to healthy stress management and your willingness to improve over time, you send a giant signal to the young ones observing you. Give yourself a few moments to relax and reduce your own stress in a healthy way before interacting with children.

Beyond setting a good example, adults can engage children in a two-step, stress management process.

1. Help children become aware that stress is affecting them in a given situation. This awareness is mindfulness at work!

2. With compassion, offer ideas for healthy methods of dealing with stress.

The first step is to *help children become aware that something is stressing them out.* This simple step of acknowledging the stress may seem obvious or trivial, but it is a critical first step because it lays the foundation of mindfulness. Children are continuously learning to differentiate between their positive and negative thoughts, feelings, and behaviors, as well as those that are automatic versus those that are intentional and deliberate. By encouraging children to notice signals their bodies are sending them and to put words to their experiences, we engage them in mindfulness.

As we help children to identify stress, we go a million miles by simply listening, validating their experiences and feelings, and affirming them regardless of what they are going through. We can reassure children that big feelings like anger, fear, loneliness, or anxiety are a normal part of being human. By letting children know that stress is a natural response to challenges and uncertainty and that it happens to everyone on occasion, we remove stigma and shame around stress. The last thing anyone needs is to feel stressed about being stressed!

This brings us to step two, which is to *introduce healthy methods for dealing with stress.* This book is chock-full of these methods in the form of age-appropriate activities and lesson plans. The following section offers additional activities for soothing the nervous system.

Engaging the Parasympathetic Nervous System

Contemporary research and advanced neuroimaging technology continue to elucidate that cognitive changes can occur through the practices of mindfulness and meditation, such as variations in brainwave activity. Changes in the brain directly influence nervous-system activity.

The task we face is to temper the activity of the sympathetic nervous system with that of the parasympathetic nervous system. Listed below are simple action items we can build into our daily routines to foster relaxation. As you try these, observe how results come quickly. Your nervous system wants to switch gears and will react almost immediately.

Nervous System Soothers

- The act of sitting still, even for one complete breath cycle, can calm the mind and body.

- Gentle and purposeful movement, such as stretching or shaking, can soothe nerves as well. Mild, tranquil exercises such as yin yoga or tai chi can stimulate rest and digestion. A relaxed, ten-minute walk after a meal is another tried-and-true method.

- Slow, rhythmic breathing exercises are plentiful in this book and signal to the body that it is safe, and it is time to rest and recover.

- Singing, humming, and chanting stimulate the vocal cords and facilitate long, slow exhalation, which signals to the body that it can relax.

- Engaging in prosody (the nuances and patterns of rhythm and sound used in poetry and music) can greatly influence our nervous systems. Try speaking slowly, rhythmically, and melodically when reading poetry or telling stories to children.

- The very act of laughing aloud (even if there is nothing to laugh at) can release tension. Watch a funny movie or read a joke book and be silly enough to laugh aloud.

- Interestingly, cool water also triggers relaxation. This can be achieved by splashing cool water on your face, drinking a cold beverage and letting your tongue be immersed in it before swallowing, or a cold shower; even a minute of cold at the end of your hot shower does the trick.

When working with children, encourage curiosity and receptivity in the face of challenge. What works for them? Empower children to identify their favorite methods for easing out of a stress response. This element of choice puts them in charge of their wellness. It shows them that they have ultimate autonomy in managing themselves.

A lifelong ability to manage stress is founded in education, awareness, and self-compassion. It is then maintained through a sense of personal agency: a belief in one's own ability to confront, manage, and dissolve stress. Our goal as adults, parents, and educators is to help children learn to help themselves.

Final Thoughts

We hope this book has provided you with a solid foundation to help children practice mindfulness, learn about themselves, and engage with the world with self-empowerment and relative ease. The skills you help children to nurture through these activities will be with them for life.

In addition to sharing with children, we hope you will integrate some of these practices into your own daily life. Adults need to unravel their thoughts and feelings just as much as children, if not more. Allow yourself to be a child again, to be playful and open to finding new ways of giving up stress, finding ease, and feeling joy in everyday moments.

Notes

4. The Five Mindfulness Stepping Stones

1. "What is Mindfulness?" Mission Be, accessed August 2021, https://missionbe.org/what-is-mindfulness/.

2. "The Mind's Eye," University of Rochester, accessed February 2022, https://www.rochester.edu/pr/Review/V74N4/0402_brainscience.html.

10. How the Brain Works

1. Daniel J. Siegel and Tina Payne Bryson, *The Whole-Brain Child Workbook* (Eau Claire: PESI Publishing and Media, 2015).

2. Katherine Weare, "Evidence for the Impact of Mindfulness on Children and Young People," April 2012, https://mindfulnessinschools.org/wp-content/uploads/2013/02/MiSP-Research-Summary-2012.pdf.

11. Social and Emotional Learning

1. "Social and Emotional Learning," California Department of Education, last reviewed September 23, 2021, https://www.cde.ca.gov/eo/in/socialemotionallearning.asp.

12. Mindfulness at School

1. "What is Mindfulness?" Mission Be, accessed August 2021, https://missionbe.org/what-is-mindfulness/.

13. The Nine Intelligences

1. Howard Gardner, *Frames of Mind: The Theory of Multiple Intelligences* (New York: Basic Books, 1983).

14. Stress and Its Antidote

1. "Childhood Stress," KidsHealth, reviewed February 14, 2015, https://kidshealth.org/en/parents/stress.html.

2. "Understanding the Stress Response," Harvard Health Publishing, July 6, 2020, https://www.health.harvard.edu/staying-healthy/understanding-the-stress-response.

3. Michael D. De Bellis, Abigail Zisk, "The Biological Effects of Childhood Trauma," *Child and Adolescent Psychiatric Clinics of North America* 23, no. 2: 185-222, https://doi.org/10.1016/j.chc.2014.01.002.

Mindfulness Resources & Bibliography

Books

Gardner, Howard. *Frames of Mind: The Theory of Multiple Intelligences.* New York: Basic Books, 1983.

Kaiser Greenland, Susan. *Mindful Games.* Boulder: Shambhala Publications, 2016.

McKeever, S.G. *7 Secrets to Super-Health: Powerful Lessons in Personal Change.* San Diego: McKeever Publishing, 2000.

McKeever, S.G. *Learn to Meditate.* San Diego: McKeever Publishing, 1997.

McKeever, S.G. *Learn to Teach Meditation and Mindfulness: A Comprehensive Guide and Scripting for Meditation Teachers.* San Diego: McKeever Publishing, 2021.

McKeever, S.G. *Paths are Many, Truth is One: A Journey to the Essence of Spirituality and Religion.* San Diego: McKeever Publishing, 1998.

McKeever, S.G. *Strategy for Success: An Outline for Personal Growth.* San Diego: McKeever Publishing, 1993.

McKeever, Sujantra and Andrew A. Kutt. *America's Heroes and You: Celebrating America's Peacemakers.* San Diego: Pilgrimage Publishing, 2001.

Roberts, Lisa. *Teach Your Child Meditation.* New York: Sterling Publishing, 2014.

Siegel, Daniel J. and Tina Payne Bryson. *The Whole-Brain Child Workbook.* Eau Claire: PESI Publishing and Media, 2015.

Verde, Susan. *I Am* book series. Accessed September 2021. https://www.susanverde.com/susans-books.

Articles & Website Content

CASEL. "SEL Policy at the Federal Level." Accessed August 2021. https://casel.org/federal-policy-and-legislation/.

Cherry, Kendra. "The 4 Stages of Cognitive Development." Updated March 31, 2020. https://www.verywellmind.com/piagets-stages-of-cognitive-development-2795457.

De Bellis, Michael and Abigail Zisk. "The Biological Effects of Childhood Trauma." *Child and Adolescent Psychiatric Clinics of North America* 23, no. 2: 185-222. https://doi.org/10.1016/j.chc.2014.01.002.

Department of Education, California. *Preschool Learning Foundations, Volume 1*. Sacramento: CDE Press, 2008. https://www.cde.ca.gov/sp/cd/re/documents/preschoollf.pdf.

Department of Education, California. "Social and Emotional Learning." Last reviewed September 23, 2021. https://www.cde.ca.gov/eo/in/socialemotionallearning.asp.

Harvard Health Publishing. "Understanding the Stress Response." July 6, 2020. https://www.health.harvard.edu/staying-healthy/understanding-the-stress-response.

KidsHealth. "Childhood Stress." Reviewed February 14, 2015. https://kidshealth.org/en/parents/stress.html.

Mission Be. "What is Mindfulness?" Accessed August 2021. https://missionbe.org/what-is-mindfulness/.

Pilgrimage of the Heart Yoga. https://pilgrimageyoga.com/.

Weare, Katherine. "Evidence for the Impact of Mindfulness on Children and Young People." April 2012. https://mindfulnessinschools.org/wp-content/uploads/2013/02/MiSP-Research-Summary-2012.pdf.

Made in the USA
Columbia, SC
20 April 2023

15627997R30057